Everybody's Historic
London

Also by Jonathan Kiek

Everybody's Historic England

Everybody's Historic London

A History and Guide

Jonathan Kiek

Foreword by Fred Housego

Maps and Drawings by David Cheepen

Published in association with SUN LIFE

Quiller Press
London

For Lynda, Timothy and Miranda

First Published 1984
by Quiller Press Ltd
46 Lillie Road
London SW6 1TN

Reprinted 1985, 1986, 1988, 1990, 1997

ISBN 1 899163 21 2

Jonathan Kiek, who has studied history and London all his life, is now a teacher and historian.
David Cheepen, who has worked as an architectural draughtsman, now has paintings and drawings in over 200 private collections round the world.

Designed in association with Book Production Consultants

Phototypeset by Hobson Street Studio Ltd,
44a Hobson Street, Cambridge CB1 1NL

Printed in Hong Kong

Contents

Acknowledgements

M y father suggested this project, and my mother typed the manuscript. Their help was invaluable. My wife gave constant support and encouragement. John Fisher at the Guildhall Library made my task easier at the time and has continued to keep me abreast of developments. This book would have been the poorer without Tom Picton's photography, and others lent a hand in different ways. I owe a considerable debt of gratitude, not least to London's historians both past and present.

Jonathan Kiek

Cover illustration: Opening of Tower Bridge, 1894. (Courtesy – Bridgeman Art Library)

Foreword

When another book on London arrives, one must assume that the author has attempted to solve that age-old conundrum – how to get a quart into a pint pot. If so, Mr Kiek has succeeded with style. He has managed to present old facts and new in an entertaining and lucid fashion. The suggestions for further reading allied to recommended day-tours will be invaluable to people discovering London for the first time. My only regret is that I didn't write it!

Fred Housego

When a man is tired of London he is tired of life; for there is in London all that life can afford.

Dr Samuel Johnson

In 1810, Sun Life opened its doors for business at Bank Buildings, opposite the Bank of England in the City of London. With nearly 200 years' experience Sun Life continues to be one of the most important institutions in the square mile.

It is appropriate that this progressive financial services organisation should be associated with this outstanding guide to London which outlines the centuries of history behind its development. Essentially a practical guide, the day tours open up to visitors, and many Londoners, the opportunity to find for themselves the visual traces of London's long history.

7

Introduction

Historic London is for everybody, but it's hard to know where to begin. *Everybody's Historic London*, which is both a concise history and a guide, is intended to help. Each chapter covers an historical period and is followed by mainly guide material relating to that period. The age of a building's brick or stone is often less memorable than its historical association so, to take an example, the largely 19th century neo-Gothic Palace of Westminster is placed with the medieval chapter. Physically, in fact, our London is largely the creation of the Victorians and their successors. The speed of the process perplexed the Victorians. In 1873 a journal commented that 'Old London, London of our youth, is becoming obliterated by another city which seems rising up through it as mushrooms do in a sward'. There are many today who feel the same about the London of their youth, which the *Luftwaffe* during the War and property developers since have helped to transform. In the face of the mushrooming office-blocks, Historic London is increasingly important to everybody – or should be.

There are plenty of guides available. If it's the full picture you want, I recommend the Penguin and Blue Guides. Among the many others, there are the Baedeker (the new not comparable to the old), the Red Guide, the Nicholson Guides, and two 'Essential Guides' by David Benedictus and Hunter Davies (published by Sphere and Pan respectively). In a different category, William Kent's *Encyclopaedia of London* (Dent) is a gold-mine for antiquarian particulars. For architecture there are the two London volumes of Pevsner's *The Buildings of England* and the GLC's mammoth *Survey of London*. There are informal guides such as the *Companion Guide to London* by David Piper (Collins), *In Search of London* by H. V. Morton (Methuen) and Harold P. Clunn's pre-war *The Face of London* (Spring Books). A practical guide to the distinctive localities is the *Observer's* 1977 symposium, *Village London*. There is Egon Ronay for the purely gastronomically inclined. Then there are the human guides. Most, like the Yeoman Warders (Beefeaters), know their patches well, but a few don't. Look out for the blue badge (the London Tourist Board accreditation). Wearers could well be members of The Guild of Guide Lecturers.

John Stow's *Survey* (1598) – available in an Everyman edition – and Sir Walter Besant's late-19th century volumes are still fascinating historical quarries. For modern scholarship readably distilled there is the Secker and Warburg series. Volumes include *The Shaping of a City* by Christopher Brooker and Gillian Keir and *Hanoverian London* by George Rudé. Much of the scholarly work has been appearing since 1856 in *The Transactions of the London and Middlesex Archaeological Society*. The stream of popular, often large and, sometimes, glossily insubstantial books on London will never run dry. An excellent compact history was Robert Gray's *A History of London* (Hutchinson). *London: 2000 Years of a City and its People* by Felix Barker and Peter Jackson (Cassell, Papermac) was a valuable addition to the list because of its wealth of illustrations and its highlighting of historical maps and views. *London as it might have been* by Felix Barker and Ralph Hyde (John Murray) will be even more fascinating if you know something about London as it is. The aerial perspective was described by Alistair Cooke with Robert Cameron (*Above London*, Bodley Head).

Everybody's Historic London is a discriminating beginner's course with the 'field work' – the twenty tours – coming at the end, when something has been learned of what the *Observer's Village London* described as 'the most surprising and varied city in the world, a tapestry of well-defined villages, each one with its own attractions, community and character'. Oliver Wendell Holmes wrote that no person can be said to know London. This is true, but a start can be made.

Jonathan Kiek

Note

See page 242 for a selection of general books on London published since 1984.

1 Landmarks in the History of London

43	Start of Roman Conquest of Britain; bridge built over Thames
61	First London destroyed by Boudicca
c.200	Building of wall
410	Withdrawal of Roman Army
604	First St. Paul's
851	London destroyed by Vikings
886	Alfred recovers London from Vikings, then repairs walls
1014	London Bridge pulled down on orders of King Olaf, attacking in alliance with Ethelred
1016	(Traditionally) Cnut tries to capture London by constructing a canal round the bridge on the south bank
1050	Start of rebuilding of Westminster Abbey by Edward the Confessor
1066	The Battle of Hastings; later, Londoners carry their surrender to William at Berkhamsted
1078	Building of White Tower begun
1979	William I grants London's first charter
1176–1209	Building of first stone London Bridge
1191	Formation of the Commune
1193–1212	Mayoralty of Henry Fitzailwin
1269	Consecration of Westminster Abbey (present building)
1348	Black Death strikes London, killing about one third of inhabitants
	Cemetery built on future site of the Charterhouse
1371	Founding of the Charterhouse
1381	The Peasants' Revolt
	The Savoy Palace burned down
1391–1419	Richard Whittington mayor four times
c.1422	Building of the Guildhall completed
1476	Caxton sets up the first printing press in England near the Chapter House of Westminster Abbey (later moved to 'the Sign of the Red Pale' by the Almonry)
c.1483	Presumed murder of the Princes in the Tower

*c.*1500	The earliest painting of London, showing the Tower, London Bridge and the City
1529	Fall of Wolsey
	York Place (renamed Whitehall) and Hampton Court acquired by Henry VIII
1535–1539	Dissolution of Monasteries, including Westminster Abbey; land made available for th future development of London
1550	Incorporation of Southwark into the City of London as 'The Ward of Bridge Without'
*c.*1550	Wyngaerde's *Panorama* – the first panoramic view of London
*c.*1559	Earliest map of London (most probably lost original, engraved on copper, of later woodcut map attributed to Agas)
1561	The spire of Old St. Paul's burned down
1568	The Royal Exchange
1580	Royal proclamation against building outside city gates
*c.*1585	Shakespeare arrived in London
1586	Staple Inn
	Publication of Stow's *Survey of London*
1598	Timbers of the Theatre in Shoreditch ferried across to Bankside to make the Globe
1603	Death of Elizabeth I at Richmond
1614	The New River
1622	The Banqueting House (Indigo Jones)
1629	William Newton obtains licence to build houses round three meadows called Lincoln's Inn Fields
1632	Development of Covent Garden begun
1642–1646	London in First Civil War; new wall and fortifications
1649	Charles I executed outside the Banqueting House
1652	First Coffee House in St. Michael's Alley, Cornhill
1663	First Drury Lane Theatre
1665	The Great Plague
1666	The Great Fire
1667	The Rebuilding Act
1670	Drawings for new St. Paul's submitted by Wren
1671	Attempted theft of the Crown Jewels by Colonel Blood
1674	Second Drury Lane Theatre by Wren
1677	The Grosvenor estate founded by the marriage of Sir Thomas Grosvenor and Mary Davies
1687	Death of Nell Gwynn at a house in Pall Mall
1694	The Bank of England begins life in Mercer's Hall, Cheapside

1698	Whitehall Palace largely destroyed by fire
1705	Opera House in the Haymarket (on site of present-day Her Majesty's)
1710	Building of St. Paul's completed
1718	Wren's Custom House destroyed by fire
1726	Guy's House
1733	The Fleet covered
1737	Johnson and Garrick set out for London
1740	Sadler's Wells Theatre
1747	The Foundling Hospital
1756	The New Road (the modern Marylebone, Euston and Pentonville Roads)
1764	Death of Hogarth
1766	The Theatre Royal, Haymarket
1768	The Royal Academy
	'The Massacre of St. George's Fields' – eleven Wilkite rioters shot by troops
1768–1772	Building of the Adelphi
1773	The first Stock Exchange building
1774	John Wilkes Lord Mayor
1775	Buckingham House purchased by George III for Queen Charlotte
1776	Garrick's farewell performance at Drury Lane
	Dr Johnson has dinner with John Wilkes
1780	The Gordon Riots
1787	Opening of the first Lord's cricket ground on future site of Dorset Square (just north of the New Road)
1794	The Third Drury Lane Theatre
1801	First census – London's population just under one million
1802	Gaslighting first demonstrated in Soho
	The West India Docks (first large wet docks)
1810	The start of the Regency
1811	Marylebone Park becomes available for development, and John Nash's scheme is accepted
1812	The fourth Drury Lane Theatre
1814	Gaslighting installed permanently in Piccadilly
	Lord's moved to its present site in St John's Wood
1817	First Waterloo Bridge
1818	The Old Vic (then the Coburg)
1819	First Southwark Bridge
1826	University College – the 'godless' institution of Gower St.
1829	Shillibeer's horse-bus service inaugurated – Paddington Green to the Bank via the Angel, Islington
	The Metropolitan Police Force – 'the Peelers'

1829–1841 Trafalgar Square laid out
1831   New London Bridge (sold to Americans in 1969)
1834   The old Palace of Westminster largely destroyed by fire
1836   Southwark to Greenwich railway opened as London's
          first passenger railway
1843   Nelson's statue placed in Trafalgar Square
          Sir Marc Brunel's Rotherhithe tunnel (first tunnel under the
          Thames, now serving the Whitechapel-New Cross line)
1844   The Oval cricket ground laid out with turf from Tooting
          Common
1845   Completion of the British Museum in the grounds of
          Montagu House
1851   The Great Exhibition
1855   First post box on the corner of Fleet St. and Farringdon St.
1858   The 'Great Stink'
1861   The Tooley Street fire (worst fire since 1666)
1863   Start of the Metropolitan line
1864   First Peabody building (in Commercial Street, Spitalfields)
1864–1870 Building of the Victoria Embankment
1866   The Metropolitan Fire Service – a direct result of the
          Tooley Street Fire
1869   The Albert Embankment
1870   Death of Charles Dickens
1874   Destruction of the Jacobean Northumberland House, next
          to Charing Cross station, to make way for
          Northumberland Avenue, linking the Victoria
          Embankment and Trafalgar Square
          The Chelsea Embankment
1878   Gate at Temple Bar removed to Hertfordshire
          Arrival of Cleopatra's Needle
          First large-scale street lighting using electricity on the
          Embankment
1879   First telephone exchange on Coleman Street
1881   First electric lighting of a theatre (the Savoy)
1888   Jack the Ripper in Whitechapel
          First big electric power station at Deptford
1889   Creation of London County Council
          The Docker's Strike – 'The Docker's Tanner' won; first
          important victory by a modern trade union
1890   The first tube – from the City to Stockwell
1891   First volume of Charles Booth's survey, *Life and Labour*
          of the People of London
1894   Building of Tower Bridge with double drawbridge
          First Lyons teashop, at 213 Piccadilly

1897	Queen Victoria's Diamond Jubilee
1901	Death of Queen Victoria
	First electric tram (Hammersmith to Kew)
1905	First fleet of motor buses (horseless carriages)
	Opening of Aldwych and Kingsway, linking Strand and Holborn
	Start of Harrods in Brompton Road
1909	Gordon Selfridge opens department store in Oxford Street
1911	The Sidney Street siege
1913	The first Chelsea Flower Show
1915	First zeppelin over City drops bomb near Guildhall
1922	London's first broadcast from Marconi House in Strand
1923	BBC moves into Savoy Hill, off Strand
	The first FA Cup Final at Wembley Stadium
1926	General Strike
1931	Shell-Mex House, Embankment
1932	Broadcasting House, Portland Place
1935	Green Belt established by LCC
	Battersea power station (Sir Giles Gilbert Scott)
1936	Battle of Cable Street
	Destruction of the Adelphi
1938	Finsbury Health Centre – postwar London architecture foreshadowed
1940–1941	The Blitz
1943	The County of London plan
1951	The Festival of Britain
1959	London Wall linking Moorgate and Aldersgate Street
1963	The Shell Building completed
1965	Creation of the Greater London Council
	Post Office Tower (580 feet, with 40-foot mast – at this time the tallest building in Britain)
1967	Centre Point
1973	Completion of new Stock Exchange
	New London Bridge
1974	Covent Garden Market moves to Nine Elms
1976	The National Theatre (Denys Lasdun, architect)
	The Notting Hill Carnival riot
1977	Silver Jubilee of Queen Elizabeth II
1980	The Iranian Embassy siege
1981	National Westminster Bank (over 600 feet – the tallest building in Britain until Canary Wharf)
	Labour takes control of the GLC under the leadership of Ken Livingstone
	Cheap fares introduced

1981	The Brixton Riots
	The first London Marathon
1982	Fares raised 100 per cent after Law Lords rule Cheap Fares Scheme illegal
	The Barbican Centre
1983	Lady Mary Donaldson becomes the first woman Lord Mayor
1984	Parliament debates the proposed abolition of the GLC
	The St. James's Square siege
	Official opening of the Thames Barrier
1985	Fire at Hampton Court Palace
1986	GLC abolished
	New Lloyds building in the City (Richard Rogers, architect)
1987	Fire at Kings Cross
	Docklands Light Railway – a fast service between the City and the Isle of Dogs
	The London City Airport
	Excavation of the Roman Basilica
1987–1990	Building of Canary Wharf
	Continued exodus of newspaper and printing firms from Fleet Street
1988	Excavation of Roman London's amphitheatre next to the Guildhall
	Clapham Junction Rail Disaster
	Sainsbury Wing, National Gallery
1988–1989	Excavation of the Globe Theatre in Southwark
1988–1990	Broadgate Development (Liverpool Street Station)
	Rebuilding of Little Britain
1989	The Marchioness Tragedy
1989–1990	Rebuilding of Charing Cross Station
1990	Ludgate Hill Rail Viaduct removed giving clear view of St. Paul's
	The Courtauld Institute moves to Somerset House
1991	Queen opens new Liverpool Street station and Broadgate development
1992	St. Mary Axe bomb wrecks Baltic Exchange
1993	St. Ethelburgh's Church wrecked by bomb
	M16 Headquarters
1994	Rail service through the Channel Tunnel commences
	Waterloo international terminal opened
1995	VE day celebrations
1996	Opening of reconstructed Globe Theatre, the brainchild of Sam Wanamaker
1997	First books moved to new British Library site in St Pancras
	State funeral of Diana, Princess of Wales.

2 Roman London

For the settlers and traders of early times the Thames was the main gateway to Britain. There were farming communities in the London area over 3,000 years before the arrival of the Romans. A bronze-working industry had grown up, flourished for almost a millenium, then declined. Heathrow had for a while been a place of considerable importance, a religious centre with a wooden temple in the classical style. But the Romans were the first to take advantage of the river-site where the City of London was to grow up.

The invasion of Britain commenced, on the instruction of the Emperor Claudius, in AD 43 when Aulus Plautius landed at Richborough in Kent with 40,000 soldiers. During the early campaigning, a bridge – no doubt a temporary structure at first, most likely consisting of boats lashed together, but soon to be made permanent – was constructed across the Thames, then a comparatively shallow river with extensive marshes, particularly along the southern shore. The bridge was a vital crossing-point on the overland route from the Channel ports to *Camulodunum* (Colchester), the city which Claudius had decided to make his capital. London, at first a supply depot for the Roman army, grew up around the bridge, mainly on the northern side. Here the terrain included two pieces of convenient high ground on either side of a stream, the Walbrook. (The name is Saxon, meaning 'the stream of the British'.) Near Cannon Street station there's a dip in the road before the ascent to St. Paul's. It was here that the Walbrook flowed down to the Thames. The first settlement, very small in extent, was built on Cornhill, to the east of the stream.

It was the Thames which brought about the rise of *Londinium*. Ships from the continent would enter the estuary and sail up as far as the bridge, purposely located just beyond what was then the river's tidal limit. What was almost certainly a foundation pier of that bridge was recently unearthed by archaeologists. The road from it ran north along the line of what is now Fish Street Hill to the

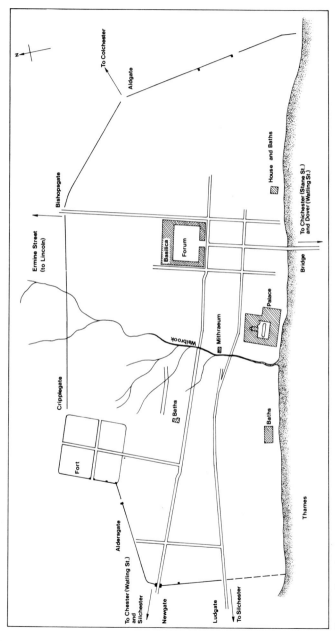

Roman London

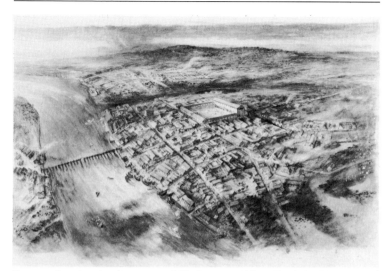

Roman London in the reign of Hadrian c. 120 A.D. (The Museum of London)

forum. After the initial period the city port was militarily insignificant. The Roman historian Tacitus writes that in AD 61 London was full of merchants and their wares, but was undefended by ramparts.

A layer of dark red ash about fifteen feet below the present street-level is all that remains of this city, the one destroyed by Boudicca in AD 60 when, according to Tacitus, 70,000 Londoners were slaughtered, a figure probably not greatly exaggerated. Some coins fused by the flames have been found near London Bridge. The next city spread from Cornhill across the Walbrook westwards to Ludgate Hill, where St. Paul's now stands. Before the end of the first century, London had superseded Colchester as the leading centre of the Roman province of Britain. A pointer is the fact that Classicianus, appointed Procurator of Britain shortly after the Boudiccan revolt, was buried here. The Hadrianic fire of *c.*125, despite being a major disaster – as is shown by the extent of the burnt pottery unearthed on both sides of the Walbrook – was only a temporary reversal, though it probably didn't seem so at the time.

As well as being its greatest port, London was the hub of the province's system of communications. Ludgate took the traffic using Akeman Street, which led via the line of the Strand through Kensington and Hammersmith to join the Silchester Road at Chiswick. Newgate was the exit for traffic using the Silchester

19

The Roman City wall in the course of construction c. 200 A.D. (The Museum of London)

Road, following the line of Holborn, Oxford Street and Bayswater Road. The Roman Watling Street from Richborough and Dover to Chester (not to be confused with the Saxon Watling Street from St. Paul's churchyard to Queen Street) crossed the Thames at the Westminster ford. To the north it followed the line of the Edgware Road. Between Westminster and Marble Arch, where Edgware Road starts, no part of the street has been discovered. Ermine Street led north through Bishopsgate by the line of Kingsland Road on its way to Lincoln. The road to Colchester left the city at Aldgate, the route being represented by Whitechapel High Street. Stane Street (to Chichester) followed the line of Kennington Park Road, Clapham Road and Tooting High Street.

The wall, which dates from about AD 200, was roughly two miles long, probably twenty to twenty-five feet high, and seven or eight feet thick. It consisted mainly of ragstone, which was quarried in the Maidstone region and then brought down the Medway and up the Thames. The remains of a barge, which still contained its ragstone cargo, was found near Blackfriars Bridge in 1962. The vessel must have sunk before delivering its load.

Extended, heightened and restored, the wall was to protect

London for fourteen centuries. Parts of it may be seen today. In the north-west corner, well away from the built-up area, was a rectangular fort with two intersecting roads and corner towers. This was the standard pattern of Roman forts. Its north gate was the original Cripplegate. Wood Street follows the road which ran up the middle of the fort. The centre of the fort was where Wood Street meets Addle Street, which follows the line of the fort's east-west road. In London, as in all Roman towns, the streets were laid out at right angles to each other like a chess-board, each space occupied by a square block called an insula. But it was the Roman wall, and not the Roman grid, which would shape the city's long-term future.

The focal point of Roman London, serving as town hall and lawcourts, was the basilica,* a species of secular cathedral with a nave and an east and west aisle, and colonnades of pillars dividing the nave from the aisles. Situated on the summit of Cornhill, its southern aisle formed one side of the *forum*, an open courtyard about four times the size of Trafalgar Square, and bounded on the other three sides by offices and shops, their goods displayed on open counters. Today Leadenhall market occupies the site where once the diverse inhabitants of a city port – Gauls and Spaniards as well as Britons and Romans – met to discuss anything from the weather to pressing provincial affairs. They were only a short walk from the Governor's Palace, built between AD 80 and 100, and discovered during the building of Cannon Street station. It was fronted by a quay that has been excavated to the south of Thames Street. An amphitheatre was excavated next to The Guildhall in 1988.

London was well endowed with baths. There were public ones in what is now Cheapside, opposite St. Mary-le-Bow Church, and another bathing-complex was in Upper Thames Street. Private baths were common among the wealthy; one of them has been unearthed in Lower Thames Street. 'Baths, wine and women corrupt our bodies,' wrote one Roman, 'but these things make life itself.' According to Tacitus, his father-in-law Agricola (governor from AD 77 to 83) built baths in order to civilize the British.

Religious observance was as important as bathing in the daily life of Roman Londoners. Apart from the compulsory emperor worship, there were cults to the Olympian gods such as Apollo and Venus, as well as to indigenous deities such as the three Celtic Mother-Goddesses. The many finds in the Walbrook suggest that the stream

---

* Test trenches dug on the site in 1985 indicated archaeological remains an amazing three metres thick. The site was fully excavated in 1987.

was sacred, people coming to it to make their offerings. A further discovery, made in 1954, was a temple of Mithras (*Mithraeum*) on the present site of Bucklersbury House, Walbrook. In design it is like a Christian church with a central nave, aisles and apse. Mithras was the Persian god of heavenly light, his cult being one of the mystery religions which came from the East. Its adherents, many of them soldiers, formed a secret society with initiation rites. Until the third century Mithraism more than rivalled Christianity, yet although there is no evidence that any existing city church is of Roman origin, it is certain that Christianity had followers in London, for in 314 a Bishop of London attended the Council of Arles, which was summoned by Constantine following his recognition of Christianity as a legal religion within the empire.

In 410 the Roman soldiers left Britain never to return. London didn't collapse, however. The house in Lower Thames Street, where a private bath has been excavated, was occupied long after the Romans had left. Initially the Saxons kept away from the city, found in their settlements at a distance ('-ham', '-ton' and '-ing' are common endings of Saxon place-names). When London emerged from the obscurity of the Dark Ages (in 604 it receives a mention in the *Anglo-Saxon Chronicle*), it flourished because it continued to be, as in Roman times, a port and the centre of a road system – in Bede's words 'a mart of many peoples'.

Further Reading

The Excavation of Roman and Medieval London W. F. Grimes (Routledge, 1986)

The Roman City of London Ralph Merrifield (Benn, 1965)

Roman London Ralph Merrifield (Cassell, 1969)

London, City of the Romans Ralph Merrifield (Batsford, 1983)

Roman London Alan Sorrell (Batsford, 1969)

Roman London Peter Marsden (Thames & Hudson, 1980)

3 Historic London (1)

The Governor's Palace

Nothing visible survives of what was probably the palace belonging to the Roman Governor of Britain. It was a vast building with an ornamental pool in its courtyard, standing near the mouth of the Walbrook on the present site of Cannon Street station.

The Roman and Medieval Wall

The Roman wall around the City, about two miles long, seven or eight feet thick, and probably twenty to twenty-five feet high, was built AD *c.*190–225 with ragstone shipped along the River Medway from Maidstone. It was repaired and partly rebuilt for the last time in the 15th century. There were seven Roman gates including the north and west gates of the fort. Moorgate was built in the Middle Ages. There was a late Roman riverside wall destroyed before Fitzstephen's time (12th century) by the action of the river.

A large section of the Roman and medieval wall of London can be seen in **Wakefield Gardens** beyond Tower Hill underground station. Note the bands of tiles in the Roman layer, which survives to a little above ground level. Nearby is the bronze replica statue, with funerary inscription, of Classicianus, the Roman Procurator of

Remains of the Roman and medieval wall in St. Alphage's Churchyard (City) near the Museum of London (Guildhall Library, City of London)

Britain who successfully opposed the harsh policy adopted by Suetonius Paullinus, the Governor, after the defeat and suicide of Queen Boudicca. Classicianus appealed to the Emperor Nero, not normally associated with clemency, and he had Paullinuis replaced. The original tombstone of Classicianus is in the British Museum.

Another section of the wall may be seen south of Midland House in **Cooper's Row**. Again, the upper part is medieval. The name of the modern street, **London Wall**, is misleading inasmuch as it follows the route only from Broad Street to Moorgate. At the Museum of London there is a special viewing window over the section in the churchyard of St. Alfage, where the wall becomes one with that of **The Roman Fort**, built AD 120–30 and discovered in 1950. Note the thickening added to the inner side of the earlier fort wall to produce the same thickness as the city wall. The west gate of the fort is in Noble Street.

See Nikolaus Pevsner's *The Buildings of England: London*, volume 1, for a full description of the wall and its making.

The Temple of Mithras

Built on the east bank of the Walbrook sometime after AD 200, the temple of Mithras was unearthed in 1954 beneath the foundations of Bucklersbury House, and later reconstructed in the forecourt of the Legal and General Assurance Society's building (Temple House) in Queen Victoria Street. Its treasures may be seen at the Museum of London. In design like a basilica or church, the stubs of pillars dividing the nave from the side aisles have survived.

London Stone

Look, in Cannon Street, at the modern wall of the Bank of China, for embedded in it is the far older London Stone, thought by some to have been the *milliarium* of Roman London, from which the distances on the Roman roads were measured. Camden, the Tudor antiquarian, wrote: 'On the south side of this high street [Candlewick or Cannon Street] near unto the channel, is pitched upright a great stone, called London Stone, fixed in the ground very deep . . . The cause why this stone is set there, the time when, or other memory, is none.' About a century later the great stone was already reduced to a stump.

Mosaics

The two mosaics in the Bank of England may only be seen by special permission. The one found in Leadenhall Street, showing Bacchus riding on a panther, is on display in the British Museum.

The Roman Bath

Situated near the Strand, off Surrey Street, this is a disappointment – it's only *alleged* to be Roman. Adjacent are the remains of an Elizabethan bath, said to date from 1588.

4 Medieval London

Though the Romans founded the original city, it was above all the monarchs who created the modern capital. Edward the Confessor took the decisive step when he built the royal Palace of Westminster on the Isle of Thorney; Henry VIII took another when he dissolved the monasteries which for centuries had restricted the city's expansion. When James I helped to finance the New River Scheme, he unwittingly facilitated the growth of the northern suburbs. Two centuries later, the partnership of the Prince Regent (the future George IV) with the architect John Nash had a notable effect on the development of central London.

Between the City of London, which grew rich because of its port, and the monarchs, who made the City of Westminster their seat of power, a mutual hostility existed for centuries. The reported remark of a twelfth century citizen that 'London will never have any king but the mayor' was only marginally an overstatement.

The Tower of London, built by William the Conqueror, was intended to cow the City, but far from being cowed, it played an active part in toppling kings from their thrones. The spirit of independence has not died, nor have the ancient and colourful traditions associated with the square mile.

There is a famous description of medieval London by William Fitzstephen, a monk who was with Becket at the time of his murder in 1170. He begins with an encomium:

> 'Amid the noble cities of the world, the City of London, throne of the English kingdom, is one which has spread its fame far and wide . . . It is blessed by a wholesome climate, blessed too in Christ's religion, in the strength of its fortifications, in the nature of its site . . .'

He continues with a precise rendering of the topography:

> On the east lies the royal citadel, of very notable size and

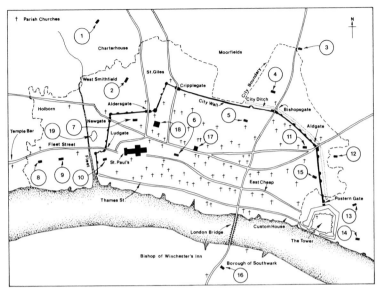

Chaucer's London

1. Priory of St. John of Jerusalem
2. Priory of St. Bartholomew
3. Hospital of St. Mary Spital
4. Hospital of St. Mary of Bethlehem
5. Austin Friars
6. St. Mary-le-Bow
7. Grey Friars
8. Temple
9. Whitefriars
10. Blackfriars
11. Priory of Holy Trinity
12. Abbey of the Minoresses
13. Abbey of Mary Graces
14. Hospital of St. Katherine
15. Crutched Friars
16. Hospital of St. Thomas
17. Mercers' Hall
18. Goldsmiths' Hall
19. Fleet Prison

strength . . . On the west are two keeps strongly fortified [the castles of Baynard and Montfichet] . . . The whole way round the north of the city the wall, tall and wide, strengthened with turrets at intervals, links the seven gates of the city. [Ludgate, Newgate, Cripplegate, Aldersgate, Bishopsgate, Aldgate and the Tower postern – Moorgate was not added until the 15th century]. Once London was walled and towered on the south side too, but that great river, the Thames, well stocked with fish, with tidal flow and ebb, has lapped against the walls over the years and undermined and destroyed them.

Two miles to the west of the City, with a populous faubourg [suburb] in between, the royal palace [of Westminster] rises on the bank, a building of the greatest splendour with outwork and bastions. Everywhere without their houses are the citizens' gardens side by side yet spacious and splendid, and set about with trees. To the north lie arable fields, pasture land and lush, level meadows, with brooks flowing amid them, which turn the wheels of watermills with a happy sound. Close by is the opening of a mighty forest, with well-timbered copses, lairs of wild beasts, stags and does, wild boars and bulls.

There are also in the northern suburbs of London splendid wells and springs, with sweet, healing, clear water . . . Holywell, Clerkenwell and St. Clement's Well are especially famous and often visited; and crowds of schoolboys and students and young men of the City take the air there on summer evenings . . .

In Fitzstephen's London most houses were of one storey, timber-framed, with walls of wattle and daub. Smoke from the wood fire issued through a hole in the thatched roof. Wooden shutters served instead of glazed windows. As in Roman London, stone houses belonged only to the wealthy, such houses being surrounded by large gardens 'well furnished with trees, spacious and beautiful'. Fire was a constant hazard. It repeatedly damaged and in 1136 totally destroyed the timber London Bridge. Generally, things weren't so rosy as Fitzstephen portrayed them. A Winchester monk, Richard of Devizes, was struck mainly by London's vice and crime, including the crowds of pimps. 'All sorts of men crowd together there from every country under the heavens. Each race brings its own vices and its own customs to the city.' His warning was: 'If you do not want to dwell with evil-doers, do not live in London.'

Around the time Fitzstephen wrote his biography of Becket, Peter de Colechurch, formerly chaplain of the church where Becket was christened, started to build a stone London Bridge, sited between the wooden bridge and the present bridge, and running from near St. Magnus Martyr in Lower Thames Street to St. Olave's. It still wasn't finished when he died in 1205. On the bridge was the chapel of St. Thomas à Becket, where the pilgrims bound for Canterbury would halt to pray, though at the Reformation it was turned into a grocer's shop. Some blocks from Colechurch's construction, which remained in use until the early 19th century, may be found in the churchyard of St. Magnus Martyr. It was supported by twenty piers, or starlings, each shaped like a boat. There were stone gates at each end and a towered gate in the middle from which a drawbridge was operated. Though splendidly durable, the bridge had

The first stone London Bridge. To the left is the newly constructed bridge of 1831 (sold to the Americans in 1969) (Guildhall Library, City of London)

one disadvantage. The piers obstructed the flow of the Thames, creating a torrent – navigating these rapids, or 'shooting the bridge' in a small boat was dangerous – and, upstream, between Westminster and the City, a pond which tended to freeze over. This circumstance made possible the rare and famous Frost Fairs, when stalls and even printing presses were set up on the ice. A fund was set up for the upkeep of the bridge, which was for several centuries administered from a house on the south side called Bridge House – hence Bridge House Estates, which today are run by a committee of the Corporation. From this source the building and repair of the four City bridges has been financed.

The outlook of the medieval Londoner was dominated by religion. There was an abundance of churches – Fitzstephen counted 126 within and without the wall – and they were the focal points of the city's growth in the 11th and 12th centuries.

Besides the churches, there were the religious houses, such as Holy Trinity Priory by Aldgate and the Convent of St. Helen's Bishopsgate, founded in 1212, shortly after Fitzstephen's time. The naves of the convent church and of the more ancient parish church exist alongside each other today, separated at the west end by Perpendicular arches and at the east end by arches of an earlier period.

The friars arrived in the 13th century. The Franciscans (the Grey

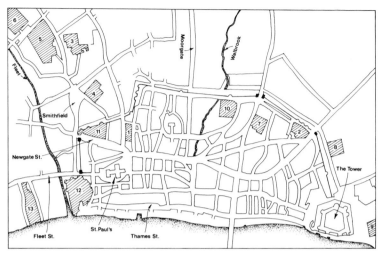

The Monasteries of medieval London

1. St. Martin's-le-Grand
2. Priory of the Holy Trinity
3. Charterhouse
4. Priory of St. Bartholomew
5. Priory of St. John of Jerusalem
6. Clerkenwell Nunnery
7. St. Helen's Priory
8. Abbey of St. Clare
9. St. Katherine's by the Tower
10. Priory of Austin Friars
11. Greyfriars
12. Blackfriars
13. Whitefriars

Friars) first had a house in Cornhill, then moved to Newgate, where they built the magnificent Christ Church, probably the largest church in England. It was destroyed in the Great Fire, rebuilt by Wren, then again destroyed in 1940. The division between the church's choir and nave is marked by Greyfriars Passage off Newgate Street. The Dominicans, or Black Friars, first established themselves in about 1221 near Lincoln's Inn, moving about fifty years later to what is now Blackfriars Lane, to the north of Blackfriars Bridge. The Carmelites, or White Friars, established themselves nearby in 1241. These foundations were after Fitzstephen's time, but the monk knew the Hospital and Priory of St. Bartholomew, Smithfield, which was found by Rahere, a courtier of Henry I. The Norman priory church of St. Bartholomew the Great exists today – but only in part. What is now the gateway to the churchyard was originally the west end of the church, the present church comprising not much more than the choir of the original. The remains of the old nave's columns are by the pavement which leads to the porch. North of Smithfield are the remains of another, and much later, priory. This was Charterhouse, a Carthusian foundation of 1371.

Of course, the City hardly offered seclusion. Outside the wall, away from the hubbub, was Westminister Abbey with its vast estates. To the south of the river stood St. Saviour's Bermondsey, a Cluniac foundation of the 11th century – and the Augustinian priory of St. Mary Overie, which was responsible for the hospital of St. Thomas's (now in Lambeth). Clerkenwell contained both a nunnery and the English headquarters of the Knights Hospitallers, whose church was burned down by the peasants in 1381. The gatehouse and the priory church crypt – today part of St. John's church, which incorporates both the Romanesque (Norman) and Gothic styles – still survive.

Fitzstephen's city was divided into twenty-four administrative wards. This number became twenty-five with the creation of the Ward of Farringdon Without in 1394. Each ward was under an alderman, whose main function was to keep the peace; even today, every alderman is by virtue of his office a justice of the peace. The wards were like miniature hundreds (the judicial divisions of the county) with the equivalent of hundred courts. Their origin was Saxon, and was probably connected with the defensive system organized against the Danes. For this reason the wards, unlike the parishes, included land on the outer side of the wall. These are still the administrative divisions of the city. The largest of them are on the periphery, where the population in Saxon times was most sparse.

The first, and unelected, mayor (the term 'Lord Mayor' was not used until the fifteenth century) was Henry Fitzailwin, a powerful personality who, supported by his aldermen, ruled the roost until his death in 1212. Meanwhile, a rift was growing between the governors and the governed. This resulted from the formation of the Commune, or self-governing municipality, in 1191. The commune took over taxation, so that the oppressors of the poor were no longer royal officials but the Corporation – the mayor and the aldermen, who elected the mayor. The aldermen themselves were elected by the wards, though they controlled these elections in their own interests. In 1196 a goldsmith, William Fitzosbert, known also as Longbeard, led a popular revolt. After putting it down, the City authorities smoked him out of St. Mary-le-Bow, where he had gone for sanctuary, then hanged him.

The lack of a trade in medieval London brought not only the possibility of starvation, but also exclusion from citizenship with its attendant rights to vote and to trade without restriction. Only by practising a trade could an inhabitant of Chaucer's London obtain membership of a guild, and thereby access to the Freedom of the City. Thus guild membership offered both social status and economic security. A trader from outside the City, whether from Bristol or Lombardy, was viewed as a rival. If Englishborn, they were classified as 'foreign'. If born overseas, they were described as 'alien'. Hatreds were fierce. In 1456 some Italians were killed in a brawl which led to the temporary expulsion of the whole community. The merchants of the Hanse were also on the receiving end when, in 1493, the steelyard was invaded by a mob of 500 Londoners who set fire to the building. Not until the 19th century did the Common Council abolish all restrictions on trading by non-freemen.

The origins of the guilds are the religious fraternities of Anglo-Saxon times. For a long time they were neither primarily concerned with trade, nor confined to those in the same trade, though this was the established pattern by Chaucer's time. Even so, their religious and social functions continued to be important. Originally, it was only by serving an apprenticeship that one could join a guild, but by the fifteenth century membership could also be purchased and in-herited, or presented free of charge to weighty individuals, who did not need to be practising merchants. As a result, guilds eventually ended up with only nominal involvement in the activity signified by their titles. The crafts, as they were also called, were not equally rich and powerful. The merchant guilds, like the mercers and goldsmiths, had an importance denied to the handicraft guilds like the potters and weavers. Rivalries were often intense, and regularly resulted in street fights between the apprentices, for centuries a barely containable section of the City's population.

The powerful crafts were the first to buy royal charters and thus become livery companies, so called because of the gowns, or liveries, which they were now allowed to wear – though from the 15th century these were worn by only the substantial members (the liverymen). The so-called Great Twelve – in order of precedence, the Mercers, Grocers, Drapers, Fishmongers, Goldsmiths, Skinners, Merchant Taylors (in alternate years, Merchant Taylors, Skinners – hence the phrase 'sixes and sevens'), Haberdashers, Salters, Ironmongers, Vintners and Cloth-workers – survive as such to this day. There are also over seventy minor companies.

At the beginning of the 14th century London was still governed by a landowning oligarchy of twenty-four aldermen, elected in the wards. Naturally, the crafts wanted to wrest power from this élite and control the City in their own interest. Their ambition was

The Arms of the Great Twelve livery companies (Guildhall Library, City of London)

achieved, but it was the liverymen of the Great Twelve – the merchant capitalists, not the craftsmen and shopkeepers – who took control. One élite had merely replaced another. From the ranks of this governing group the mayor and sheriffs were elected by the citizens in Guildhall.

Since 1475 the sheriffs have been elected by the liverymen, acting on behalf of the citizens, in an assembly that came to be known as 'Common Hall'. It is all that has survived from the Folkmoot, the popular assembly of Saxon origin. Since 1585 this election has taken place on Midsummer Day. On Michaelmas Day (29 September) the liverymen assemble once more, this time to nominate two aldermen for the mayoralty. The final choice is made on the same day by the Court of Aldermen. Before the election a service is held at the Corporation church of St. Lawrence Jewry next to Guildhall. The aldermen themselves, like the Common Councilmen, are still elected in the wards. In the middle of the last century the freedom, with its right to vote, was made automatically available to everyone on the Parliamentary register of the City. Since then the number of residents has become very small, though there has been some increase in post-war years. Like the vast majority of medieval Londoners, the modern commuting population is without representation. This could change – in February 1984 the Court of Common Council was debating whether to enfranchise 6,000 shopkeepers and bankers. (The honorary freedom, which is occasionally conferred by the Court of Common Council on the great and famous, is quite different from the ordinary freedom, which is simply citizenship.)

In Geoffrey Chaucer's time about a quarter of the City's working population belonged to guilds. Below the level of the humblest guilds – and also of the labourers in regular employment, such as the domestic servants and Thames boatmen – there was the inevitable substratum of wretchedness and criminality. Many of the rogues and beggars found their way to Westminster where they sought the charity of the monks. Over the river lay Southwark, where criminals found refuge because it lay outside the jurisdiction of the City. The needs of travellers and pleasure-seekers were served by the borough's plentiful inns and brothels. Among the former were 'that high class hostelry known as the Tabard, close beside the Bell', the meeting-place of Canterbury pilgrims.

Dirt and disease usually go with poverty, but everyone suffered from the scanty provision for sanitation and refuse collection. The Thames was both a depository for all types of refuse and a source of water supply. Water was also drawn from wells befouled by the overflow of the cesspits. Fortunately, there were several public fountains, most notably the Standard and the Great Conduit in Cheapside, bringing clearer water from the Tyburn, Paddington and Highgate. The depression in the middle of the cobbled street was both a gutter and depository for trade and household waste, though not all of it ended up there. Each ward had rakers, whose wages were collected and paid by a scavenger. Not all rakers took their duties seriously. One in Cheapside used to push the dung and filth from his own ward into the adjacent one of Coleman Street, until he was prosecuted for anti-social activity. A dung agent was hired to empty the cesspits, an office performed at night. The cesspits were usually outside, though in the best houses there would be one under the cellar floor with a pipe to the privy above. In official circles concern about sanitation showed itself in a stream of regulations. In 1345, for example, a two shillings fine was imposed on anyone casually throwing dirt and rubbish onto the streets. In 1354 there was an ordinance to keep pigs from wandering. The most unpleasantly smelling area was probably the criminal neighbourhood of the polluted Fleet river. Sadly for both convents of friars, which were situated to either side of it, the filthy upper reaches above Holborn Bridge, which polluted Farringdon Without downstream, lay outside the control of the City's authority. The White Friars, though accustomed to earthly discomfort, were moved to complain of the stench, but action on the Fleet was not to be taken until much later, after the Great Fire. It required the cholera outbreaks of the mid-19th century to bring about fundamental reform in London's sanitation.

The poor were vulnerable to the Black Death, which struck London in November 1348, but this virulent outbreak of the bubonic plague, carried by rats brought to England in ships' cargoes, was no respecter of high degree. At Westminster the abbot perished with most of his monks. Another to die was Sir John Pulteney, four times mayor. Some 20,000–30,000 people died altogether – a third of London's population. New cemeteries had to be built to accommodate them, including one north of Smithfield where Charterhouse, a Carthusian monastery, was later built. During the next three centuries plague was to visit London on a number of occasions. The Great Plague of 1665, so vividly described by Pepys, was by no means extraordinary. Unfortunately, the earlier outbreaks missed the eye of a great diarist.

Let's imagine a walk through the late-14th-century London which Geoffrey Chaucer knew. The area within its walls is less than a square mile, and the suburbs without are still small. It's like a country town. Approaching from the east through the cornfields of Bethnal Green and Stepney, we enter the City at Aldgate. Chaucer, who is controller of the wool custom and subsidy in the port of London, is living in rented accommodation above this gate. Each day he hears the sound of horses and carts bound for the markets. Each night he listens to Bow Bell ringing the curfew, to warn people that the gate will soon be shut.

Londoners live by buying and selling, in the markets and in the smelly streets where pigs and other animals roam freely. (Lovat Lane, near the Monument, recalls these narrow, cobbled streets with their central gutters.) The shops with their protruding signs are very small. Above them are the brightly painted timber-framed homes, often with pointed gables, whose upper storeys, three or more becoming common, tend to overhang the street. (A 17th century example of a similar house is to be found today in Cloth Fair, near Smithfield Market.) The tradesmen are generally also craftsmen, who produce the goods they sell. As in Roman times, their workroom is at the back of the shop, goods being displayed on the open counter at the front. When night falls, wooden shutters will be put up.

From East Cheap, scene of a lively market, we go to Lombard Street, colonized by the Italian bankers, the Crown's chief money-lenders following the expulsion of the Jews by Edward I. Passing through the Stocks, a meat and fish market and site of the city stocks (where now the Bank of England stands), we arrive in Poultry, to the east of Westcheap, or Cheapside, the main shopping centre of medieval London, outstanding for its width in this city of narrow streets. Instead of the usual booths on either side, there is sometimes the gorgeous spectacle of a royal tournament, the fashionable spectators sitting in a stone gallery constructed against the north wall of St. Mary-le-Bow. This was built by Edward III for Queen Philippa, who had been hurt when the earlier wooden gallery collapsed in 1329.

The following lines from Lydgate's *London Lackpenny* written in the early fifteenth century, give an idea of Cheapside's atmosphere:

> Then to the Chepe I began me drawn,
> Where much people I saw for to stand:
> One offered me velvet, silk and lawn,
> Another he taketh me by the hand:
> 'Here is Paris thread, the finest in the land.'

It's usual in medieval London for men in the same line of business to congregate together. For example, the saddlers are found in Foster Lane and the candlemakers in Candlewick (Cannon) Street. (Names like Poultry, Milk Street and Ironmonger Lane indicate their medieval associations.)

The tall spire of old St. Paul's, the largest building in England, soars heavenwards, reaching 450 feet (nearly a hundred feet higher than the cross on top of Wren's St. Paul's). In the north-east corner of the walled churchyard, ancient meeting-place of the Folkmoot, which has long since declined into nominal life, is an ornamental cross above an octagonal wooden pulpit. This is Paul's Cross, the regular and official place for public pronouncements – '*The Times* newspaper of the Middle Ages', as Thomas Carlyle described it. Following the perimeter of the churchyard, we go along Paternoster Row, the street of the text-writers and rosary-makers, or paternosterers, then make our exit at Ludgate, where a prison is attached, as there is at Newgate. On our left, within the city wall, is the convent of the Blackfriars. Ahead on our right, outside the City wall, is the Fleet prison. Reaching for our handkerchiefs, the smell here being somewhat unpleasant, we cross the Fleet Bridge, then continue along Fleet Street, passing the convent of the Whitefriars to our left. (A vault from the prior's house may be reached from a building in Britton's Court, off Whitefriars Street). On our right we come to the church of St. Dunstan-in-the-West (which is still there today), then to a bar across the road. This is Temple Bar which, like Holborn Bar to the north, divides the City from Westminster. The dignity of the buildings on the river side of the Strand attracts us. Here are bishops' palaces and the fine Savoy Palace, home of the mighty John of Gaunt. (The chapel of the Savoy, south of the Strand near Waterloo Bridge, occupies part of the site today.)

*Preaching at Paul's Cross – 'The Times Newspaper of the Middle Ages'.
From a picture dated 1616* (Guildhall Library, City of London)

Soon we come to the small village of Charing. Here stands the last of Edward I's memorial crosses erected to his beloved wife, Queen Eleanor. Turning left along a muddy lane, later to become Whitehall, we pass York Place, which Henry VIII will make the nucleus of Whitehall Palace. The track brings us to the heart of Westminster which is dominated by Abbey and Palace. Here our walk ends.

By Chaucer's time Westminster had become the settled seat of government. The administrative machinery had once accompanied the King on his peregrinations. Winchester was the capital or *caput regni*, because it was the favourite residence of the sovereign, but the organs of government were not permanently settled there. When the King moved on, they went with him. Henry III (1216–72) wished to remain for long spells in the Palace of Westminster, where he could involve himself in the rebuilding of the Abbey. This explains why the entire work of government came to be done at Westminster, though the process was interrupted in the reign of Edward I. During his Welsh campaigns government moved to Shrewsbury and, during the later campaign against the Scots, to York. If Scotland had been conquered, York rather than London might have become the capital of Britain. Fortunately for the inhabitants of Westminster, who complained bitterly about the loss of wealth caused by the absence of bureaucratic patrons, the Hundred Years War, which ended any possibility of the conquest of Scotland, made certain that London would develop as England's capital. In 1338 Edward III ordered the Exchequer to leave York for Westminster 'so that it might be nearer to him in the ports beyond the sea'. Later it was joined by the judges of the King's Bench and Common Bench, and by the clerks of the Court of Chancery. Judges and Chancery clerks sat in different corners of Westminster Hall. The clerks, whose religious vows entailed the communal life, were eventually to occupy a house on the site of the Public Record Office in what became Chancery Lane.

Further Reading

Medieval London Timothy Baker (Cassell, 1970)
The Shaping of a City, London 800 to 1216 Christopher Brook and Gillian Keir (Secker & Warburg, 1971)
Norman London Sir Frank Stenton (included in *Social Life in Early England,* ed. G. Barraclough *[Routledge, 1960]*)

Medieval London: from commune to capital   G. A. Williams (Athlone Press 1963)

The Rulers of London in the 12th Century   Susan Reynolds (*History*, October 1972)

Chaucer's London   D. W. Robertson (Wiley, 1968)

The Turbulent London of Richard II   Ruth Bird (Longman, 1949)

The Merchant Class of Medieval London   Sylvia Thrupp (Cambridge, 1948)

Medieval Westminster, 1200–1540   Gervase Rosser (Oxford: Clarendon Press, 1989)

5 Historic London (2)

Westminster Abbey

The Tyburn, one of London's lost rivers, forked to form Thorney Isle before it reached the Thames. According to tradition a church was built on the island by Sebert, King of the East Saxons, and consecrated by Mellitus, first Bishop of London in 616. The first historical record is of the Benedictine abbey, founded in the eighth century by King Offa of Mercia and dedicated to S. Peter – although it received the name 'West Minster', or western monastery, because of its position to the west of the city. Edward the Confessor rebuilt

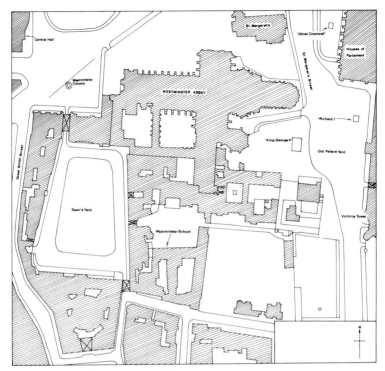

The Environs of Westminster Abbey

the abbey, consecrating it on 28 December 1065. On 6 January 1066 he was buried there. The Bayeux Tapestry shows his body being conveyed on a bier towards a church with a tower and round Norman arches. To indicate its recent completion, a weathercock is being placed on the roof. Within this Norman church, or its mainly Early English successor, every sovereign since William I (except Edward V and Edward VIII) has been crowned. Henry III (1216–72) decided to honour St. Edward by rebuilding the entire church.* In 1269 it was consecrated, though the nave was not actually finished until the early years of the 16th century. From the reign of Henry III until George III chose to be buried at Windsor, the abbey was the chief burial church of English monarchs.

Enter by the west door. The **Nave** is the highest in England – 103

---

* Henry was influenced by churches he had seen in France (such as the Sainte-Chapelle in Paris). Pevsner described the abbey as 'the most French of all English Gothic churches.'

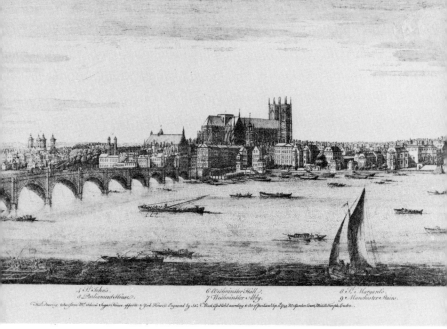

An 18th century engraving of Westminster (Guildhall Library, City of London)

feet. The slab of marble inscribed 'Remember Winston Churchill' was placed here on the twenty-fifth anniversary of the Battle of Britain. **The Tomb of the Unknown Warrior** was brought from Flanders and interred here on 11 November 1920 to represent all the nameless British dead in the First World War. Look for the portrait of Richard II, the oldest contemporary portrait of any English monarch. Eight pairs of windows on the north side of the nave each show the figure of a different king and his contemporary abbot of Westminster.

In the **North Aisle** of the **Nave** look for a small stone in the pavement which, inscribed 'O Rare Ben Johnson' (*Sic*), marks the grave of the poet Ben Jonson (1573–1637). The monuments, busts and floor-slabs crowd in on you. This is, after all, as much a national museum as a church. No political party has a monopoly. One of the monuments is to Spencer Perceval (1762–1812), the Prime Minister shot in the House of Commons.

The **Choir Screen** was erected 1833–4. For revealing nature and its laws Sir Isaac Newton has his monument in the left recess. Stop and reflect that daily services have been sung on the site of this choir for 900 years.

In the **North Choir Aisle** don't miss a series of medallions under

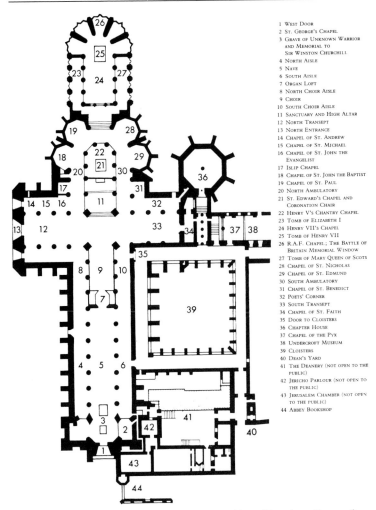

1 WEST DOOR
2 ST. GEORGE'S CHAPEL
3 GRAVE OF UNKNOWN WARRIOR
   AND MEMORIAL TO
   SIR WINSTON CHURCHILL
4 NORTH AISLE
5 NAVE
6 SOUTH AISLE
7 ORGAN LOFT
8 NORTH CHOIR AISLE
9 CHOIR
10 SOUTH CHOIR AISLE
11 SANCTUARY AND HIGH ALTAR
12 NORTH TRANSEPT
13 NORTH ENTRANCE
14 CHAPEL OF ST. ANDREW
15 CHAPEL OF ST. MICHAEL
16 CHAPEL OF ST. JOHN THE
   EVANGELIST
17 ISLIP CHAPEL
18 CHAPEL OF ST. JOHN THE BAPTIST
19 CHAPEL OF ST. PAUL
20 NORTH AMBULATORY
21 ST. EDWARD'S CHAPEL AND
   CORONATION CHAIR
22 HENRY V'S CHANTRY CHAPEL
23 TOMB OF ELIZABETH I
24 HENRY VII'S CHAPEL
25 TOMB OF HENRY VII
26 R.A.F. CHAPEL; THE BATTLE OF
   BRITAIN MEMORIAL WINDOW
27 TOMB OF MARY QUEEN OF SCOTS
28 CHAPEL OF ST. NICHOLAS
29 CHAPEL OF ST. EDMUND
30 SOUTH AMBULATORY
31 CHAPEL OF ST. BENEDICT
32 POETS' CORNER
33 SOUTH TRANSEPT
34 CHAPEL OF ST. FAITH
35 DOOR TO CLOISTERS
36 CHAPTER HOUSE
37 CHAPEL OF THE PYX
38 UNDERCROFT MUSEUM
39 CLOISTERS
40 DEAN'S YARD
41 THE DEANERY (NOT OPEN TO THE
   PUBLIC)
42 JERICHO PARLOUR (NOT OPEN TO
   THE PUBLIC)
43 JERUSALEM CHAMBER (NOT OPEN
   TO THE PUBLIC)
44 ABBEY BOOKSHOP

A plan of Westminster Abbey Westminster Abbey (Receiver General)

the organ, and three matching diamonds in the pavement. They commemorate English scientists and composers respectively.

In the **North Transept** the party political flavour of the monuments is particularly strong. You are in '**The Statesmen's Aisle**'. Here the statues of Gladstone and Disraeli, bitter rivals in their day, are forced to keep each other's company.

In The Sanctuary, which is the raised space within the altar rails,

Fan-vaulted Henry VII's Chapel, Westminster Abbey (Guildhall Library, City of London)

there are three beautiful tombs, dating from the late 13th and early 14th centuries. The altar and reredos were designed by Sir Gilbert Scott in the 19th century.

The **Coronation Chair** in St. Edward's Chapel was made to enclose the **Stone of Scone** which Edward I purloined from the Scots in 1926.* The chapel contains, apart from the shrine of St. Edward, the tombs of Henry III, Edward I and his wife Eleanor of Castile, Edward III and his wife Philippa of Hainault, and Richard II and his first wife Anne of Bohemia.

The **Henry VII Chapel**, built 1503–19, is the finest example in England of late-Perpendicular Gothic. Stop to admire the tall windows and the fan-tracery vaulting. Then look for the tombs of Henry VII, Elizabeth of York, (his wife) and Elizabeth I.

In the **South Transept** and **Poets' Corner** there are wall-paintings of *St. Christopher* and *The Incredulity of St. Thomas* attributed to Walter of Durham (about 1280). Find, among the tombs and gravestones of the famous, the gravestone of obscure Thomas Parr (d. 1635), 'Old Parr', who is said to have lived 152 years and under ten sovereigns.

The **Cloisters**, whose earliest parts date from the mid-13th century, are connected with the church by two doors in the south nave aisle. From the East Walk proceed to the **Norman Undercroft** or to the **Chapter House**, a beautiful octagonal room built *c.* 1245–55. The paintings on the walls depict the Book of Revelations, which Newton loved to study when not revealing nature's laws. From the South Walk you will come to the peaceful Dean's Yard, a pleasantly secluded area for picnicking. Dean's Yard leads into Broad Sanctuary, where criminals once found immunity from the arm of the law. At the start of Tothill Street, where the almonry was situated, William Caxton had his printing press from 1483.

The Palace of Westminster (1)

The Palace of Westminster was the main London residence of the sovereign from the reign of Edward the Confessor until Henry VIII expropriated Whitehall.

The House of Commons once met in the Chapter House of Westminster Abbey. The House of Lords used to meet in The Painted Chamber which stood at the south end of **Old Palace Yard**, the main courtyard of the old palace. It was in a cellar under The Painted Chamber that Guy Fawkes stored his gunpowder in 1605.

*It was returned to the Scots in 1996.

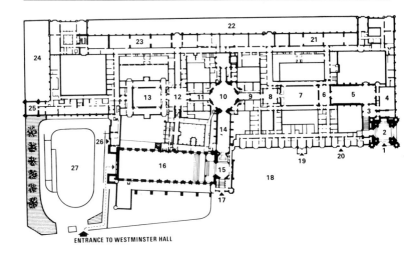

ENTRANCE TO WESTMINSTER HALL

KEY TO PLAN: *1 Royal Entrance; 2 Victoria Tower; 3 Norman Porch; 4 Robing Room; 5 Royal Gallery; 6 Prince's Chamber; 7 House of Lords; 8 Peers' Lobby; 9 Peers' Corridor; 10 Central Lobby; 11 Commons' Corridor; 12 Commons' Lobby; 13 House of Commons; 14 St. Stephen's Hall; 15 St. Stephen's Porch; 16 Westminster Hall; 17 St. Stephen's Entrance; 18 Old Palace Yard; 19 Peers' Entrance; 20 Chancellor's Gate; 21 Lords Library; 22 River Terrace; 23 Commons Library; 24 Speaker's Green; 25 Clock Tower; 26 Members' Entrance; 27 New Palace Yard.*

A limited number of seats in the Gallery of each House is available for the general public when the House is sitting. Visitors should wait outside St. Stephen's Entrance until directed to enter. The House of Lords Record Office is open from 9.30 a.m. to 5.30 p.m., Mondays to Fridays (tel. 01-219 3074).

A plan of the Palace of Westminster (Controller of Her Majesty's Stationery Office)

In 1547 the Commons were allowed by Henry VIII to move to St. Stephen's Chapel, built by Edward I, whose shape and size is represented by St. Stephen's Hall. One of the eleven courtyards is Star Chamber Court, recalling the Star Chamber, where the Court of Star Chamber (abolished 1641) held its sittings. Though there were stars on the ceiling, a likely origin of the name is the Jewish starrs, or bonds, once stored there. A model of the old Parliament buildings is in The Queen's Gallery.

Apart from the Jewel Tower, only Westminster Hall and the crypt and cloisters of St. Stephen's Chapel survived the fire of 1834. The conflagration occured when the tallies (notched sticks once used for keeping exchequer accounts) were piled into a stove in the House of Lords. The fire was stoked too vigorously with the result that nearby panelling caught alight. Soon the Palace was ablaze. The Hall, crypt and cloisters are incorporated in the present neo-Gothic building, designed by Sir Charles Barry and decorated by Augustus Pugin. It was almost a lifetime's task for both men. Barry probably died from exhaustion. Pugin went mad. Barry had favoured a classical design, the M.P. s demanded the Gothic style, the style of the old palace. The site wasn't changed partly because, as the Duke of Wellington stressed, the Thames provided a defence against the mob.

Close to the site of the clock-tower of the old palace a new clock-tower was erected. Inside it was installed a bell weighing 13½ tons (3½ tons less than 'Great Paul'). It is most likely named after a contemporary prizefighter, Benjamin Caunt, but there is some doubt because the first Commissioner of Works at the time was another Ben, a large Welshman called Sir Benjamin Hall. Big Ben was recast at Whitechapel from an earlier and even larger bell which had cracked. When this one also cracked (the crack is visible today) a lighter hammer began to be used. The chime is said to be derived from a phrase in the accompaniment to the aria 'I know that my Redeemer liveth' from Handel's *Messiah*. The Dents, father and stepson, constructed the clock and clock-tower in collaboration with the cantankerous E. B. Denison, later Lord Grimthorpe, the restorer of St. Albans Abbey.

At the other (west) end of the palace is the Victoria Tower, built by Barry to accommodate the historic documents of Parliament. There are about three million stored here today.

At night a light in the clock-tower of Big Ben (the Ayrton Light, named after another early commissioner), and during the day a flag on the Victoria Tower, indicate that Parliament is in session.

On 10 May 1941 the House of Commons was almost totally

THE NORTH-WEST VIEW OF WESTMINSTER HALL, &c.

A 19th century view of Westminster Hall (Guildhall Library, City of London)

destroyed in an air raid. The Commons moved to the ornately decorated environment of the Lords' Chamber, and the Lords to the Queen's Robing Room. A new chamber for the Commons, designed by Sir Giles Gilbert Scott, the grandson of neo-Gothic champion Sir Gilbert, was opened in 1950. The Lords could now return to their own chamber.

Westminster Hall Westminster Hall, originally erected by William Rufus in 1097–9, was an extension of the old Saxon palace. The main courtyard of the palace came to be known as the 'old' palace yard while the one in front of Westminster Hall became the 'new' palace yard. Between 1394 and 1401, mainly in the reign of Richard II, the Norman hall was given the magificent hammer-beam roof we see today. The mason was Henry Yevele and the carpenter Hugh Herland. The rebuilding included the heightening and buttressing of the walls to enable them to carry the roof, and the construction of all the present windows.

This hall being finished in the year 1398, the same king [Richard II] kept a most royal Christmas there, with daily joustings and runnings at tilt; whereunto resorted such a number of people, that there was every day spent twenty eight or twenty six oxen and three hundred sheep, besides fowl without number. He caused a gown for himself to be made of gold, garnished with pearl and precious stones, to the value of three thousand marks.

John Stow, *The Survey of London* (1598)

Law derived from the King. It was natural that Westminster Hall, a part of the royal palace, should be closely associated with the evolution of the English legal system. It was here, until the building of the law courts in the Strand in the late 19th century, that the major law courts – Common Pleas, King's Bench, and Chancery – used to sit, at first in the hall itself, later in buildings erected outside.

Great events have been enacted in Westminster Hall, notably the depositions of Edward II (1327) and Richard II (1399) and the state trials of Sir Thomas More (1535) and Charles I (1649).

Also, as John Stow wrote, 'here have they in the great hall kept their feasts, as at Christmas and such like, most commonly.' The last coronation banquet to be held in the hall was George IV's in 1820.

Look out for (i) the statues on the east and south walls, which belong to a set of thirteen statues of English kings from Edward the Confessor to Richard II executed by Thomas Canon in 1385. (ii) a brass tablet on the steps at the south end, which marks the spot where Charles I sat during his trial; (iii) a tablet on the east wall which marks the position of the door by which Charles I entered when coming to arrest the Five Members (1641).

The Jewel Tower In 1303 the Chapel of the Pyx in the abbey, where the King's valuables were housed, was broken into. The King's crown was left lying on the floor. Greater security was now deemed essential. The originally moated Jewel Tower, which stands in Abingdon Street opposite the Victoria Tower, was designed by Henry Yevele and built in the reign of Edward III (1327–77) as part of the Palace of Westminster on land which belonged to the abbey. Not surprisingly, it was much resented by the monks. The position of the tower reminds us how large the medieval palace was.

St. Margaret's Westminster

St. Margaret's church is both the parish church of Westminster and (since 1614) of the House of Commons. The present late-Perpendicular building, the third on the site, was consecrated in 1523.

Don't miss the splendid chancel window of Flemish glass. There are memorial windows to John Milton, who was married here (so were Pepys and, more recently, Sir Winston Churchill), and to Sir Walter Raleigh, who may be buried in the chancel. There is some dispute about the location of Sir Walter's remains, which may be at Sherborne in Dorset. (Milton's are at St. Giles, Cripplegate.) The modern stained-glass windows in the south aisle are by John Piper.

The Tower of London

The Norman knights, fresh from their triumph at Hastings, found themselves denied access to the City. Not wishing to fight, they contented themselves with setting fire to Southwark, and then rode up the river on the Surrey side, at last making the crossing at Wallingford. Later William occupied the royal palace at Westminster. 'He built siege-engines,' says a Norman chronicler, 'and made moles and the iron horns of battering-rams for the destruction of the city; then he thundered forth menaces and threatened war and vengeance . . .' Even the courage of the Londoners began to waver. The surrender was carried to William at Berkhamstead. Shortly afterwards, he was crowned at Westminster Abbey.

The coronation was marred by an ugly incident. The troops on guard, mistaking the crowd's acclamation for a riot, set fire to the nearby houses. The muddle and alarm infected the dignified proceedings inside the abbey. For those who were apprehensive it was an unpromising start to Norman rule. None was more apprehensive than William, who withdrew to Barking while on his orders a wooden keep was being built on an earth mound just inside the east wall of the City. This was the origin of the Tower of London, built to overawe the Londoners.

The **White Tower** we see today was traditionally begun in the year 1078. The architect was a monk named Gundulf, who also built Rochester cathedral. The exterior was restored by Wren in the 17th

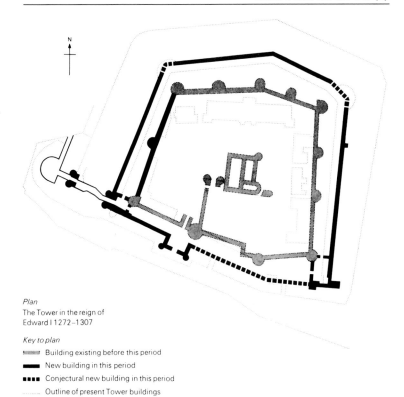

Plan
The Tower in the reign of
Edward I 1272–1307

Key to plan

▨▨▨▨ Building existing before this period

▬▬▬ New building in this period

■■■■ Conjectural new building in this period

.... Outline of present Tower buildings

The Tower of London in the reign of Edward I (1272–1307) (Controller of Her Majesty's Stationery Office)

century. The rest of the Tower dates largely from the reigns of Henry III (1216–72) and Edward I (1272–1307).

To the right of the modern entrance bridge, a bookshop occupies the site of the former **Lion Tower**, where the King's menagerie was kept until its transference in 1831 to the recently founded London Zoo at the north end of Regent's Park. The tame ravens – according to legend, the Tower will fall if it loses them – are perhaps a survival from this collection.

Pass through the **Middle Tower** and cross over the moat to the **Byward Tower**. Opposite is the **Bell Tower**, where Sir Thomas More was imprisoned before his execution in 1535. Following the **Outer Ward**, you come to **St. Thomas's Tower**, guarding **Traitor's Gate**, through which state prisoners, such as More and Anne Boleyn, were led after their trial at Westminster and short voyage down the

51

The first Painting of London (the frontispiece illustration to 'The Poems of Charles, Duke of Orleans') showing the Tower, London Bridge and the City (c. 1500). The finely dressed Duke may be seen in four places. (The British Library)

Thames. Opposite are the infamous **Bloody Tower**, traditionally the scene of the presumed murder of the little Princes, and later the prison of Sir Walter Raleigh (1604–16), and the **Wakefield Tower**, where Henry VI was found dead, believed murdered (1461). Pass under the Bloody Tower into the **Inner Ward**.

In addition to being an armoury,* the Tower also guarded – and still guards – the **Crown Jewels**. In 1671 Colonel Blood attempted to steal the jewels when they were kept in the **Martin Tower**. Charles

* Most of the armour is now in Leeds.

II pardoned Blood and even returned his confiscated estate in Ireland. (Will the full truth ever be revealed?) Apart from being a fortress, a palace (down to the reign of James I), and a state prison (as late as 1941 Hitler's deputy, Rudolf Hess, was confined in the Yeoman Gaoler's House) the Tower for a long period housed the **Royal Mint** (transferred in 1911 to a building on Tower Hill, and now at Llantrisant, near Cardiff) and the Public Records. But it is as a place of execution that the Tower is most grimly remembered. As recently as 1945, William Joyce and John Amery were hanged within its walls. Many historical figures, including Sir Thomas More, the Earl of Strafford (1641) and the Duke of Monmouth (1685), were executed on Tower Hill. A slab in Trinity Square marks the site of the scaffold. (Today Tower Hill is associated with public speaking rather than public executions – Donald Soper has missed few Wednesday lunchtimes for over sixty years). Some victims, among them Anne Boleyn and Catherine Howard, met their end on **Tower Green**. The bodies of Anne, Catherine, More and other VIP casualties lie in the **Chapel Royal of St. Peter Ad Vincula**. The timber-framed Tudor House on Tower Green is the **Queen's House**, where Anne Boleyn spent her last days, and where the Gunpowder Plot conspirators were interrogated. It was from the Queen's House that in 1716 the Jacobite Lord Nithsdale escaped in woman's clothing, so avoiding the block. Another, and

Hayward and Gascoyne's plan of the Tower of London 1597 (Guildhall Library, City of London)

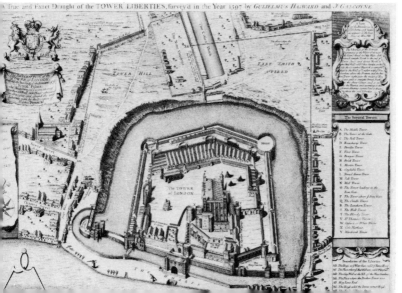

A plan of the Tower today (Controller of Her Majesty's Stationery Office)

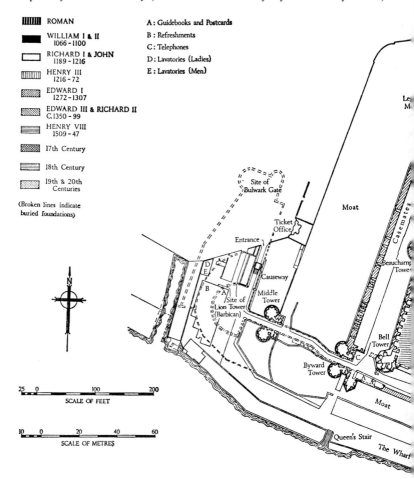

ROMAN

WILLIAM I & II
1066-1100

RICHARD I & JOHN
1189-1216

HENRY III
1216-72

EDWARD I
1272-1307

EDWARD III & RICHARD II
C.1350-99

HENRY VIII
1509-47

17th Century

18th Century

19th & 20th
Centuries

(Broken lines indicate
buried foundations)

A : Guidebooks and Postcards
B : Refreshments
C : Telephones
D : Lavatories (Ladies)
E : Lavatories (Men)

Site of
Bulwark Gate

Moat

Ticket
Office

Entrance

Causeway

Middle
Tower

Site of
Lion Tower
(Barbican)

Beauchamp
Tower

Bell
Tower

Byward
Tower

Queen's Stair

The Wharf

Moat

Casemates

25 0   100   200
SCALE OF FEET

10 0   20   40   60
SCALE OF METRES

N

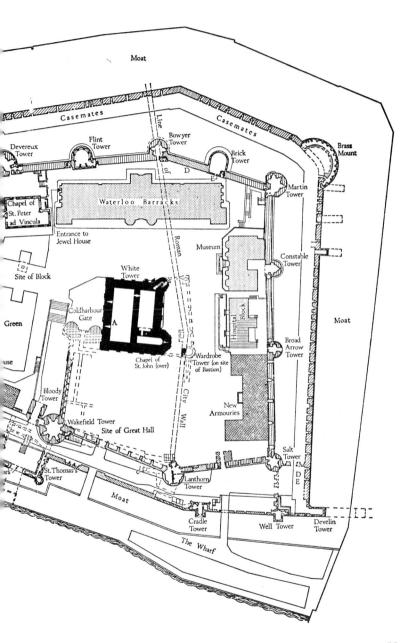

Moat

Casemates

Casemates

Brass Mount

Devereux Tower

Flint Tower

Bowyer Tower

Brick Tower

Line

D

E

Martin Tower

Chapel of St. Peter ad Vincula

Waterloo Barracks

Entrance to Jewel House

Museum

Constable Tower

Site of Block

Roman

White Tower

Coldharbour Gate

Green

A

Hospital Block

Moat

Broad Arrow Tower

Chapel of St. John (over)

Wardrobe Tower (on site of Bastion)

use

Bloody Tower

City Wall

New Armouries

Wakefield Tower

Site of Great Hall

Salt Tower

St. Thomas's Tower

D

E

Moat

Lanthorn Tower

Cradle Tower

Well Tower

Develin Tower

The Wharf

The Banqueting Floor, Entrance floor and Basement of the White Tower in Norman times (Controller of Her Majesty's Stationery Office)

later, Jacobite, Lord Lovat, was not so lucky. The block and axe used for dispatching him on Tower Hill in 1746 may still be seen. He has the melancholy distinction of being the last person to be beheaded in England. In a house next door to the Queen's House

Lady Jane Grey was confined, and from there she watched her husband, Lord Guildford Dudley, pass to the block on Tower Hill. She was executed later that day on Tower Green (12 February 1554), a victim of Tudor power-politics at its most savage.

The three diagrams show the Norman layout of the White Tower. The Basement was intended as a store but was later a dungeon. You will find the cell by the **Sub-Crypt** is aptly named the Little Ease. It was dark, unventilated and only 4ft square. In the wake of the Gunpowder Plot (1605), Guy Fawkes was tied to the floor. The entrance floor, which contains the **Crypt of St. John's Chapel**, was originally occupied by the Constable of the Tower and his soldiers.

Climb up to **St. John's Chapel**, the oldest church in London, and an example of pure Romanesque (Norman) architecture (thick pillars and round arches). Notice the different patterns at the top of the pillars. Feel the rough, honey-coloured stone. Unusually, the nave and sanctuary are undivided. Here in 1381, during the Peasants' Revolt, the rebels found Archbishop Sudbury and three others at prayer, by the altar. They were dragged to Tower Hill and beheaded. In 1554 Lady Jane Grey came here to pray on the night before her execution. To the north of the chapel was the Norman King's chamber and alongside both was the Great Hall, where the banqueting took place. Chamber and hall used to go up to the roof, as the Chapel does today.

Two ceremonial survivals deserve a mention. Every night, when he has locked the gates of the Tower, the Chief Yeoman Warder presents the keys to the Resident Governor. This Ceremony of the Keys, which may be seen with the Resident Governor's permission, goes back centuries. The ancient ceremony of Beating the Bounds takes place once every three years, when the thirty-one boundary stones of the Tower Liberty are beaten with white wands. This is a reminder that the Tower's jurisdiction once extended beyond its walls.

A warning note to end with. Get to the Tower early if you are a summer visitor, especially if you want to see the Crown Jewels speedily.

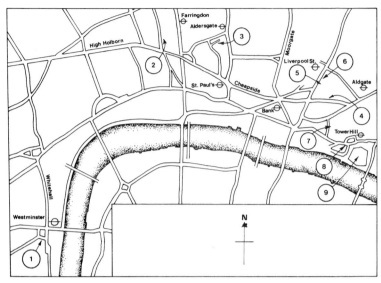

Some surviving Pre-Great Fire churches

1. St. Margaret's, Westminster
2. Ely Chapel, Ely Place
3. St. Bartholomew-the-Great, Smithfield
4. St. Andrew Undershaft, Leaden-hall Street
5. St. Helen's, Bishopsgate
6. St. Ethelburga, Bishopsgate
7. St. Olave, Hart Street
8. All-Hallows-by-the-Tower
9. St. John's Chapel (in the White Tower

Two Surviving Pre-Great Fire Churches*

The Church of St. Bartholomew the Great This superb relic of Norman London on the east side of Smithfield was founded by Rahere, a courtier of Henry I, as a thank-offering to the Almighty for bringing him through a bad illness. It seems big enough, but you are only seeing part of it; the nave of the church was demolished at the time of the suppression of the priory under Henry VIII.

Outside look for the remains of the old nave's columns. Inside find the rebus of Prior Bolton. (It consists of a crossbow-bolt piercing a cask or tun.) The prior was the architect of Henry VII's Chapel in Westminster Abbey.

* See Mervyn Blatch, *A Guide to London's Churches* (Constable, 1978)

St. John's Gate, Clerkenwell (Guildhall Library, City of London)

St. John's Gate (St. John's Lane) and St. John's Church, Clerkenwell
St. John's Gate – this isn't the original which was destroyed by the
rebellious peasants in 1381 – was the south gate of the priory of the
Knights Hospitallers of the Order of St. John of Jerusalem. The
priory, burned by the peasants, was suppressed by Elizabeth I.

St. John's church (*c.* 1720) incorporates the choir walls of the old priory church from which the crypt also dates. A line in the road indicates the area of the original nave.

Lambeth Palace

The building of Lambeth Palace was begun by Archbishop Hubert Walter (1193–1205), and since the time of his successor, Stephen Langton (of Magna Carta fame) it has been the London residence of the Archbishop of Canterbury.

Pass through the Tudor gateway, built by Cardinal Morton in the reign of Henry VII, then visit the **Great Hall**, a 17th century rebuilding in its earlier medieval style; the **Library,** whose treasures include illuminated and Elizabethan manuscripts, the letters of Francis Bacon, Gladstone's diaries and Elizabeth 1's prayer book; the **Guard Chamber,** with a reconstructed 14th century roof, containing portraits of archbishops by, among others, Holbein, Van Dyck, Hogarth and Reynolds; the **Chapel** where John Wyclif was tried in 1378, and a beautiful **Crypt,** the oldest part of the building. There is a tradition that Wyclif's followers, the Lollards, were imprisoned in the tower named after them. (The genuine Lollards' Tower, where in 1514 the London merchant, Richard Hunne, was found murdered after refusing to make a mortuary payment, was at the south-west corner of Old St. Paul's.)

Charterhouse and Smithfield

Charterhouse was founded in 1371 as a Carthusian priory. The founder was Sir Walter Manny, a soldier in the Hundred Years War, who designed it as a memorial to victims of the Black Death, thousands of whom were buried under what is now Charterhouse Square. The House was dissolved by Henry VIII, some of its monks dying for their faith at this time. From his prison window in the Tower Sir Thomas More, who had shared their uncompromising routine when a young law student at Lincoln's Inn, watched them being led on their way to Tyburn, where they were hanged and disembowelled while still alive. In 1611 the property became a school and a hostel for male gentlefolk. The school has moved to Surrey but the hostel remains.

The Late 15th century Gatehouse of Lambeth Palace (Guildhall Library, City of London)

Walk along Charterhouse Street, on the north side of the Central Meat Market, until you come to Charterhouse Square. You will see the modernized 15th-century gatehouse. The south and east walls of the **Chapel** survive from the 14th century. There is a fine 16th-century **Great Hall,** and next to it is the **Library** (17th-century), above which the **Great Chamber,** an Elizabethan room, has been restored to its former splendour.

The Charterhouse is situated north of Smithfield, originally the 'Smoothfield', boggy ground outside the city wall. Tournaments were held here regularly. Until 1855 this was the scene of Bartholomew Fair, immortalized by Ben Jonson. From the 12th century it was the chief horse and cattle market (see 'Markets'). When excavating to lay the foundations of the present market-buildings, workmen were confronted by the bones of Protestant martyrs burned here by Mary Tudor.

It was at Smithfield that Richard II met the rebel peasants led by Wat Tyler (1381). The king was accompanied by Mayor Walworth and the royal household. The catalyst of the ensuing drama was the mayor. Inevitably, the contemporary accounts of what happened are at variance. All agree that Tyler was struck by the mayor. (A replica of the offending dagger is preserved by the Fishmongers.) It seems that the mayor had previously tried to arrest him, possibly on the king's orders. A member of the royal retinue then ran Tyler through with his sword. A chronicler records he was 'carried by a group of the commons to the hospital for the poor near St. Bartholomew's, and put to bed in the chamber of the master of the hospital. The mayor went there and found him, and had him carried out to the middle of Smithfield, in the presence of his companions, and had him beheaded.'

The Borough, Southwark Cathedral and Winchester House (or Palace)

Across London Bridge, on the south bank of the Thames, lies Southwark. This bridge is new; Southwark the 'South Work' – is very old. There was a Roman settlement which has left remains. From Roman times until the mid-18th century, all the traffic to and from the Kentish ports and the south of England passed through Southwark. In medieval times it was famed for its inns, so handy for travellers when the City gates were shut. It had a hospital – St. Thomas's, which moved to Lambeth in 1865, to make way for an extension of the railway. It now has Guy's named after its founder, Thomas Guy, the son of a wharfinger in Bermondsey.

For generations the City tried to persuade the Crown to give her jurisdiction over Southwark, where her criminals lay beyond reach. Not until 1550 was the Mayor of London allowed by a charter of Edward VI to take formal 'possession' of Southwark, which became 'the Ward of Bridge Without of the City of London'. Though a ward of the City, Southwark was not allowed its own alderman. Subjection had always been the City's concern. However, the Liberty of the Clink, as the large estate of the Bishop of Winchester was known, remained independent. In Tudor times it would become London's red light district because it stayed free of the City authority's puritanical jurisdiction. The prostitutes (the 'Winchester Geese') who operated in the 'Stews' (brothels) ensured the livelihood of the Thames watermen. Other Tudor attractions were the theatres and the beer-gardens. The bishops tolerated prostitutes, who brought revenue, but not heretics, who might find themselves in the Clink prison.

The **Cathedral** is close to the bridge. Before the Reformation it was the Church of the Priory of St. Mary Overie – 'Over the river' – one of the two religious houses (the other being St. Saviour's Bermondsey) situated within the borders of the present Borough.

The choir and transepts are the original Gothic. The nave was rebuilt in the last decade of the 19th century. Behind the door into the vestry are the remains of a Norman door – all that is left of the Norman church.

The cathedral has its literary associations. There are memorials to John Gower, the poet and contemporary of Geoffrey Chaucer, and to William Shakespeare. Edmund, the brother of the bard, is commemorated by a stone in the floor of the choir.

South of the cathedral is the Borough Market established by Edward VI. Close by is **St. Mary Overie's Dock,** where the parishioners of the cathedral still retain their ancient landing rights.

Winchester House (or **Palace**) was the town residence of the bishops of Winchester, who owned the surrounding land, or manor, called the Liberty of the Clink. Don't miss the remains of the 14th-century great hall, including a beautiful rose window, now incorporated in a warehouse in Clink Street. Winchester Square nearby preserves the shape of a courtyard of the palace.

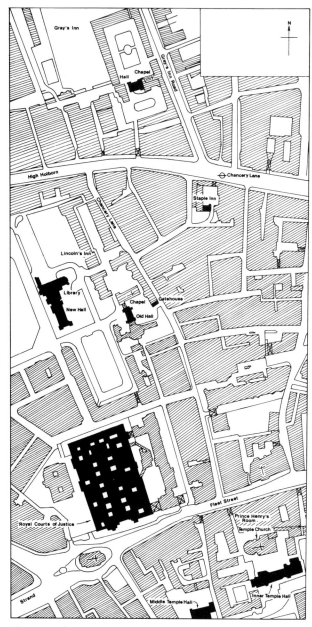

The Inns of Court

The Inns of Court

The Inns of Court – Lincoln's Inn, Gray's Inn, Inner Temple and Middle Temple – were referred to in Tudor times as 'the third university of England'. By Elizabeth's reign there were nearly 2,000 students in residence during term-time.

Lincoln's Inn Lawyers have possibly occupied the area since the reign of Edward I (1272–1307). The name is derived from Henry de Lacy, Earl of Lincoln, owner of the site and Edward I's adviser on questions of law and an advocate of legal education.

There are two halls: **Old Hall** (about 1492) and **New Hall** (1843–45) and a 17th-century **Chapel**. Both halls and chapel escaped

The 16th century Gatehouse of Lincoln's Inn (Guildhall Library, City of London)

severe damage in the Second World War. Famous members have included Sir Thomas More, William Penn, Benjamin Disraeli and W. E. Gladstone.

Don't miss the **Gatehouse** into Chancery Lane, built in 1518 by Sir Thomas Lovell, whose arms it displays.

Lincoln's Inn Fields Laid out as a square in the early 17th century, is the largest such in Central London. (see 'Historic London (4)' for Sir John Soane's Museum.) Lindsey House (No.s 59 and 60) on the west side was probably designed by Inigo Jones.

Gray's Inn owes its name to Lord Gray de Wilton, a lawyer like Henry de Lacy and once the owner of the site. Lawyers have been here since the 14th century.

The **Hall, Chapel** and **Library**, which were destroyed in the Second World War, have been rebuilt. It was in the hall that Shakespeare's *Comedy of Errors* had its first performance in 1594. Francis Bacon had chambers here from 1577 till his death in 1626.

The Temple The Temple, which extends from Fleet Street to the Thames, belonged originally to the crusading order of Knights Templars, who had their English Headquarters here.

> . . . those bricky towers
> The which on Thames' broad aged back do ride,
> Where now the studious Lawyers have their bowers;
> There whilom [formerly] wont the Templar Knight to bide,
> Till they decay'd through pride.

wrote Edmund Spenser in *Prothalamion*. The land was acquired by the Crown in the 14th century and let to lawyers. The area covers two Inns of Court: Inner and Middle Temple. The Inner is the more easterly of the two, but both lie within the City.

The Temple may be entered from Fleet Street either by Christopher Wren's Middle Temple gatehouse (1684) or through the Inner Temple gateway beneath Prince Henry's Room. **The Temple Church** shared by the Inner and Middle Temple, is one of five round churches in England, all being modelled on the Church of the Holy Sepulchre in Jerusalem. The round part was consecrated in 1185. The Early English chancel was added in 1240. The **Buttery**, at the west end of **Inner Temple Hall** (1952–6) and the **Crypt** below it date from the 14th century. (The 19th-century Hall was destroyed in the war.) **Middle Temple Hall**, with its fine

Elizabethan Middle Temple Hall with its magnificent hammer beam roof (Guildhall Library, City of London)

hammer-beam roof, dates from the reign of Elizabeth I (restored since the war). Shakespeare is said to have taken part in a performance of *Twelfth Night* here on 2 February 1601 (or 02). He describes Henry II's barons plucking the red and white roses in the Temple garden. **Fountain Court,** to the north of the Hall, was immortalized by Dickens in *Martin Chuzzlewit.* 'Merrily the fountain played and merrily the dimples sparkled on its sunny face.' This merry fountain dates from the 17th century.

Famous members of the Inner Temple have included Sir John Hampden, Judge Jeffreys and Mahatma Gandhi. Of Middle Temple – Raleigh, Fielding and Dickens. Oliver Goldsmith died in Middle Temple Lane. Charles Lamb was born in Crown Office Row. He returned to live for many years within the Temple, first in Mitre Court Buildings, later in Inner Temple Lane. Dr Johnson occupied rooms at 1 Inner Temple Lane, where Johnson's Buildings now stand.

Look out for the Winged Horse (Inner Temple) and the Lamb and Flag (Middle Temple).

The Inns of Chancery There were nine Inns of Chancery, all subordinate to the Inns of Court. Some of them now exist as names of buildings, such as **Clifford's Inn, Furnival's Inn** and **Staple Inn,** whose gabled and timbered facade (1586) may be seen in Holborn. It may previously have been a hostel for wool merchants (merchants of the Staple'). Staple Inn's two courtyards were built in the 16th century. At No. 2 in the first of these courts Dr Johnson is reputed to have written *Rasselas* in a week to pay for his mother's funeral.

Guildhall

An Haberdasshere and a Carpenter
A Webbe a Dyere and a Tapicer–

And they were clothed calle in a liveree
Of a solempne and a great fraternitee.
Well semed ech of hem a fair burgeys
To sitten in a yeldhalle on a deis
Everich, for the wisdom that he kan,
Was shaply for to been an alderman.

Prologue to *The Canterbury Tales*

The existing building, completed about 1422 in the reign of Henry V, replaced an earlier hall standing in Aldermanbury. Only the porch, the crypt and the lower part of the great hall survive. The front, except for the porch, dates from the late 18th century. The roof, destroyed in 1940, was replaced by Sir Giles Gilbert Scott.

The Guildhall, so called because it was the meeting-place of the guilds, has long been the scene of civic elections. It's also a banqueting hall. Each November, at the start of his mayoralty, the Lord Mayor entertains the Prime Minister to a splendid banquet. It was here, on Jubilee Day 1977, that the Queen was wined and dined after the thanksgiving service at St. Paul's.

The Court of Aldermen meets in Guildhall about fifteen times a year, and the Court of Common Council, consisting of the Lord Mayor, twenty-five aldermen and 130 common councilmen, at 1.00 p.m. on every third Thursday. Both meetings are public and are presided over by the Lord Mayor.

There are twenty-six wards, unequal in area and number of voters. Bassishaw, which contains Guildhall, is the smallest of

The 15th century Porch of Guildhall (Guildhall Library, City of London)

them. Each ward, except the ward of Bridge Without (Southwark), appoints one Alderman, who is automatically a magistrate, and between four and twelve common councilmen. Aldermen must be liverymen, and common councilmen Freemen of the City. Elections are known as wardmotes.

Don't miss:

(i) The city coat-of-arms over the porch. The cross is St. George's and the sword is St. Paul's. Paul is the patron saint of the City. The motto 'Domine dirige nos' means 'Lord, direct us.'

(ii) Gog and Magog

(iii) The banners hung in the roof, displaying the arms of the twelve principal livery companies. Above them are the livery shields of the lesser companies.

The Guildhall Library

The first Guildhall library was founded in the 1420's. In 1824 it was refounded as a reference library of material relating to the history of London. The new library in the west wing, opened in 1974, includes an exhibition room of books and manuscripts.

For the antiquarian-the corporation of the City of London houses its archives in the Corporation Record Office in Basinghall Street. The most celebrated item is William I's Charter to the Londoners (measuring 6 in. by 1 in.). The text begins: 'William king, greets William, bishop and Gosfrith [identified as Geoffrey de Mandeville], portreeve, and all the burghers within London, French and English, friendly . . .' The document goes on to state that the citizens would have all the rights of freemen of which they 'were worthy in King Edward's day', and that they would inherit the property of their fathers. 'And I will not endure,' concludes William, 'that any man offer any wrong to you. God keep you.'

Guildhall's medieval crypt (Guildhall Library, City of London)

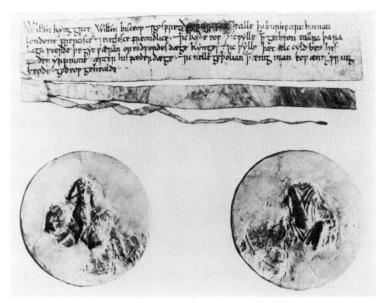

William I's Charter to the City of London (Corporation Record Office)

The Halls of the Livery Companies

Though the original medieval halls didn't survive the Great Fire, their modern successors are likely to occupy similar sites, and they may be a clue to the trade once carried out in the locality–e.g. Merchant Taylors' Hall in Threadneedle Street. Among the many others worth visiting are Goldsmiths' Hall (Foster Lane) and Mercers' Hall (Ironmonger Lane).

Contact the City Information Centre, St. Paul's Churchyard, London EC4 (tel 01-606-3030) for details of days in the year on which some of the halls are open to the public.

Crosby Hall

Crosby Hall was the great timber-roofed hall of Crosby Place, built in Bishopsgate in 1466 by Sir John Crosby, the London merchant,

The timber-roofed Hall of Sir John Crosby's House in Bishopsgate (now in Chelsea) (Guildhall Library, City of London)

'Ane of the first that adventurid into Spayn'. It was occupied by the Duke of Gloucester shortly before he became Richard III. Sir Thomas More, the garden of whose Chelsea country home included the site on which the hall now stands, moved here from the Barge in Bucklersbury in 1523. Fittingly, he wrote a biography of Richard (a damning one). The hall was brought from Bishopsgate to Chelsea in 1910 and re-erected. Humbler London houses had similar, but small-scale, halls. For example, a furrier's house (described in an early 14th-century building account) consisted of a hall with a large bay window, upper rooms, and a stable with rooms and garretts above it.

Dick Whittington* and the Whittington Stone, Highgate Hill

On a stone on this spot, marked by a stone placed here in 1821, Dick Whittington is supposed to have sat and listened to Bow Bells chiming 'Turn again, Whittington, thrice Mayor of London'. The cat was added in 1964.

Whittington, four times Mayor between 1391 and 1419, was the youngest son of a Gloucester knight. In his early teens he came to London to seek his fortune. His best move was to marry the daughter of the mercer, Sir John Fitzwarren, soon becoming Master of the Mercer's Company, then Mayor. He did business with three kings, Richard II, Henry IV and Henry V, whose bills he is supposed to have thrown in the fire, while the victor of Agincourt–his success partly due to Whittington's cash–looked on. Whittington lent for influence and business advantage where kings were concerned, and these he undoubtedly achieved, sitting on royal commissions, serving for a time on the King's Council, on one occasion being chosen by the king as Mayor, and most likely being consulted about royal policy. Henry IV gave him a licence to export wool without paying the subsidy. Twice he was collector of the wool custom and subsidy in London, a position Chaucer had held.

Latterly Dick Whittington lived alone in a vast mansion to the west of the present Cannon Street station. Nearby is the church of

* See the study, 'Richard Whittington. The Man Behind The Myth' by Caroline M. Barron. (*Studies in London History* Ed. A. E. J. Hollaender and W. Kellaway, Hodder & Stoughton, 1969).

Dick Whittington hears Bow Bells from Highgate Hill. (Guildhall Library, City of London)

St. Michael Paternoster where he was buried alongside his wife. Civic pride and a personal vanity predisposed merchants to generosity. Whittington, with no children to provide for, was more generous than most. Thanks to his munificence, Newgate Prison and the Hospital of St. Bartholomew, both in terrible state, were rebuilt. He also paid half the cost of the new Guildhall Library. We don't know whether Whittington owned a cat. It could be significant that a cat was also a coal-barge from Newcastle–and Whittington had interests in coal.

Eltham Palace

This outlying residence of monarchs was built thirteen years after Sir John Crosby's house, which may have been the model. Following the battle of Agincourt (1415) Henry V spent Christmas here before making his triumphant progress through the City. Henry VIII and Elizabeth I spent part of their childhood at Eltham.

Approach the palace by a 14th-century bridge over a moat.

Nearby are some half-timbered houses, which once belonged to an outer court. The only complete part of the palace to survive is the 15th-century banqueting hall with its fine hammer-beam roof.

Markets

Billingsgate, Lower Thames Street, EC3 Celebrated for fish and bad language, Billingsgate has Saxon origins. Only in recent centuries has it sold fish exclusively. 'A large water-gate, port or harborough for ships and boats commonly arriving there with fish, both fresh and salt, shell fishes, salt, oranges, onions and other fruits and roots, wheat, rye and grain of divers sorts for the service of the city . . .' (Stow)

The Britannia-crowned market-building, which replaced the old

The Banqueting Hall of Eltham Palace – another fine hammer beam roof (Tom Picton)

dock, is Victorian. Covent Garden started a trend–the market moved away from Billingsgate in 1982. The new site is in the West India Dock. Mr Heseltine placed a preservation order on the building.

Leadenhall, Gracechurch Street, EC3 founded in 1357 as a poultry market, Leadenhall was owned by Dick Whittington for a time before being acquired by the Common Council. The main merchants today are poulterers, though all types of food are sold here. The present buildings date from 1881.

Smithfield, Charterhouse Street, EC1 from the 12th century an annual market for livestock was held here to coincide with St. Bartholomew's Fair. It has been a regular weekday market since 1614. The present buildings were completed in 1869, some years after Smithfield had become a dead-meat market, the live market having been removed to the peace and quiet of Islington. The bones of Protestant martyrs dug up when the foundations of the Victorian structure were being laid, were a reminder that Mary Tudor (1553–8) was no favourite of the Londoners.

London Names (1)*

In the physical sense London is virtually a creation of the 19th and 20th centuries. The process of change–unceasing where the capital is concerned–can obliterate ancient associations. Names, which have proved less ephemeral than bricks and mortar, provide much of the continuity.

The random sample below all originate from the medieval period.

ADDLE STREET	From 'Adela' (filth, manure).
ALDERMAN-BURY	The first Guildhall was sited here.
ALDERSGATE STREET	Aldersgate was one of the City's seven gates. Possibly derived from a personal Saxon name, Ealdred or Aldred.
ALDGATE HIGH STREET	Stow suggested 'old gate'. In fact, the earliest known form is 'Alegate or Allgate'. Here was a famous well with supposedly curative waters. A pump was erected at the end of the 16th century. In 1876 the well was filled in, but Aldgate pump remains.
ALDWYCH	From 'eald' (old) and 'wic' (a settlement). The church of St. Clement Danes is a reminder of the Danish colony here in the 9th and 10th centuries. Danelaw (the area of Danish settlement) went right up to the walls of London.
AVE MARIA LANE	Probably from the text-writers and makers of rosaries who lived here. (See Paternoster Square)
AUSTIN FRIARS	The Augustinian Friars established themselves in London in 1253. The passage now called Austin Friars led from the gateway of the friary, on Broad Street, to the friary buildings. After the Reformation, the nave of the Austin Friars church

* See *Street Names of the City of London* E. Ekwall (Oxford), and *Discovering London Street Names* John Wittich (Shire Publications 1996)

77

was granted to Dutch Protestant refugees, and this survived till 1940. Rebuilt after the Second World War, the church is still used by the Dutch community and continues to be known as the Dutch church.

BARBICAN · A barbican was a watchtower built on a mound. By the 17th century this one was in ruins.

BAYSWATER ROAD · From 'Baynard's Watering'. Baynardus was a follower of William the Conqueror.

BASINGHALL STREET · After the town house of the Basings.

BEVIS MARKS · 'Marks' meant territory. Bevis is a corrupt form of Beris (of Bury). Hence 'the territory belonging to Bury [Abbey]', so even a distant abbey might own land in the City.

BILLINGSGATE · According to Geoffrey of Monmouth (*c.*1100–54) the name was derived from a king of the Britons called Biling. It was one of the two gates in the river wall, the other being Dowgate. Billingsgate Wharf is perhaps the oldest on the river. It was once the great port to the east of the bridge. The port gave rise to the market.

BLACKFRIARS LANE · The Dominicans, or Black Friars, who were established in about 1221 near Lincoln's Inn, moved to here about fifty years later.

BLOOMSBURY · From the Manor, or bury, of William Blemund, who acquired it in the 13th century.

CHARING CROSS · The name of the village of Charing, situated at the bend in the river, was possibly derived from the old English 'cierring' which means 'turning'. The last of Edward I's memorial crosses to Queen Eleanor was succeeded in the 17th century by the equestrian statue of Charles I. The 'Eleanor Cross' in the station forecourt is *not* a copy of the original.

CLERKENWELL · The old 'Clerks' Well was on the site of 14-16 Farringdon Road. Here the parish clerks of Clerkenwell used to perform miracle plays.

CORNHILL · Corn was probably grown here in early times.

COWCROSS STREET · This street is close to Smithfield.

CREED LANE · Probably from the text writers and makers of rosaries who lived here. (See 'Paternoster Square').

CRUTCHED FRIARS	Named after a house of the Crutched Friars, or Friars of the Holy Cross.
CURSITOR STREET	Cursitors were officials who issued writs in the Court of Chancery.
FARRINGDON STREET	Named after a 13th-century goldsmith and alderman called William Farringdon (or Farndon).
FENCHURCH STREET	A haymarket was situated near here. 'Faenum' is Latin for 'hay'. Alternatively, the medieval church of St. Gabriel was said to have been built on fenny land.
FETTER LANE	From 'fewters' (beggers) who used to gather here.
FLEET STREET	Leading from Temple Bar to Ludgate, Fleet Street crossed the river Fleet at what is now Ludgate Circus. The association with printing goes back to the late 15th century, when Wynkin de Worde set a press here.
FOSTER LANE	'Fusters' were makers of wooden saddle-bows.
FRIDAY STREET	John Stow: The street was 'so called of fishmongers dwelling there, and serving Frydayes market'.
GRACECHURCH STREET	The street was close to the grass (hay) market which may also have given its name to Fenchurch Street. It was in this street that the Quakers William Penn and William Mead were accused of causing a riot (1670). In fact they had been forced to meet in the road because they had been locked out of their Meeting House. The subsequent trial at the Old Bailey established the right of a jury to bring its verdict according to conscience.
GREAT SCOTLAND YARD	The site of the royal house, a part of Whitehall Palace, where the kings of Scotland used to stay. Here were the headquarters of the Metropolitan Police until 1811 when they were moved to New Scotland Yard, a turreted building in the baronial Scottish style near Parliament Square. Now they are in Victoria Street, where they are still known as New Scotland Yard.
GREENWICH	'Green Village'.
HACKNEY	'-ey' and '-ea' endings indicate islands above the marsh. This was Haakon's Island. There was a Danish settlement here.
HAMPSTEAD	A homestead or farm.
HARP LANE	Until the 18th century, houses and shops used signs

instead of numbers. In 1762 they were abolished for safety reasons. The sign of a harp hung from a property here.

HIGHGATE — This village is situated on high ground near Hampstead. A tollgate was erected here in the late 14th century, but this is too late to provide the origin of the name.

HOLBORN — From the 'stream in the hollow', which joined the Fleet.

HOLLOWAY ROAD — The 'Hollow-way' led from Highbury to Highgate.

HORSEFERRY ROAD — The horseferry linked Lambeth Palace on the south side of the Thames with Millbank and the Palace of Westminster on the north. The building of Westminster Bridge in the 18th century put the ferrymen out of business.

ISLINGTON — The Domesday Book (1086) refers to 'Isen' (a spring containing iron). 'Ton' denotes 'settlement'.

KENSINGTON — The Saxon Kensige family owned land here.

KNIGHTS-BRIDGE — From the bridge over the Westbourne, one of the lost tributaries of the Thames. It belonged to the knights who, before going off to war, went to Fulham to receive a blessing from the Bishop of London in the chapel of his palace.

LEADENHALL STREET — Once the site of a manor house with a lead roof.

LOTHBURY — The name probably refers to the owner of the manor (bury). Fancifully, from the loathsome smell made by founderers, pewterers and metal-workers.

LUDGATE HILL — From 'ludda' (back gate). The first reference to Ludgate Hill is in the reign of Queen Elizabeth (1558–1603).

MILK STREET — Street where milk was sold.

MINORIES — Named after the Abbey of the Minoresses, founded in 1294.

MOORFIELDS — North of the city wall was a moor or marsh. The Walbrook, which rose in these fields, overflowed and froze in the winter.

MOORGATE — The gate leading to Moorfields.

OLD BAILEY — A bailey is an enclosed area of a castle or an open space in front of a city wall. This open space in front of the wall between Ludgate and Newgate has been known as Old Bailey since the 13th century. Now the site of the Central Criminal Court.

OLD JEWRY — Originally the name of a district – 'the district formerly held by Jews.'

PADDINGTON — In Saxon times the Paeda family (ing) established a homestead (ton) here.

PANYER ALLEY STEPS — These steps leading from Paternoster Square to Newgate Street have replaced Panyer Alley, named after the basket-makers who lived here. 'Panyer' means basket. Note the sculptured figure (1688) of a boy sitting on a basket. The inscription reads:

> When ye have sought the city round
> yet still this is the highest ground.

In fact, the summit of Cornhill is slightly higher.

PATERNOSTER SQUARE — In medieval times rosary-makers, or pater-nosterers, lived here. There were also 'text writers that dwelled there, who wrote and solde all sortes of Books then in use, namely A.B.C. with the Pater Noster, Ave, Creed, Graces, etc.' (Stow).

'PETTICOAT LANE' (Middlesex Street) — Ladies' petticoats used to be sold in the clothiers' market on this site. A market still flourishes here.

POULTRY — Poultry was sold in this part of West Cheap.

QUEENHITHE — One of the ports in medieval London. A hithe is an inlet. This hithe to the west of London Bridge came under royal patronage in the 12th century. On royal initiative, London's first public lavatory was then installed here.

ST. MARTIN LE GRAND — Named after the church of St. Martin Le Grand.

SEACOAL LANE — John Stow: 'Lane where sea-coal was to be had.' The coal was unloaded at a wharf here by the Fleet.

SEETHING LANE — The name is derived from 'Ceafen', Old English for chaff. Seething Lane means 'the lane full of chaff'. The chaff may have come from the hay-market (see 'Fenchurch Street') or, more probably, from the corn that was threshed and winnowed in the lane and surrounding courts.

SOUTHWARK   The 'South Work' of the City of London. Some form of fortification is referred to.

SPITAL SQUARE   'Spital' or 'Spittle' means hospital. The priory of St. Mary Spital was founded in 1197. In the hospital churchyard stood the pulpit of Spital Cross, where the Spital Sermons were preached in Easter Week. There is still a Spital Sermon, preached these days at S. Lawrence Jewry, the corporation church.

THE STRAND   A 'Strand' is land by the sea or a river. This riverside roadway led from the City to the village of Charing.

TEMPLE   In the 12th century the Knights Templars acquired land between Fleet Street and the river. Then the area was acquired by the Crown who leased it to lawyers. From 1222 Temple Bar was the boundary post between the City and Westminster. Today the Victorian Temple Bar Memorial with its griffin marks the spot. Wren's 17th century stone gate, whose removal Victoria noted with regret on the occasion of her Diamond Jubilee, is now the entrance to Theobald's Park near Waltham Cross in Hertfordshire.

THEOBALD'S ROAD   Monarchs travelling to their palace at Theobald's in Hertfordshire took this route.

THREAD-NEEDLE STREET   Formerly Three Needles Street. It was the site of the Hall of the Needlemakers' Company, whose coat of arms includes three needles. However, the name may be connected with the Merchant Taylors, whose Hall has been here since the 14th century.

TOOLEY STREET   A corruption of Olaf, later St. Olaf, who fought with Ethelred against Cnut. It was during this successful campaign (1014) that, on Olaf's suggestion, London Bridge (being defended by Cnut's supporters) was pulled down by laying cables attached to his ships round the piles, then rowing away. Thus the rhyme at the end of the sage:

> London Bridge is falling down,
> Gold is won and bright renown.

Five City churches were dedicated to Olaf. Of

these St. Olave's in Hart Street survives.

TURNSTILE,
GREAT AND   There was a turnstile here to prevent cattle
LITTLE   straying from Lincoln's Inn Fields

WALBROOK   Named after the lost river – 'the stream of the
             Britons'.

WARDROBE   The site of the house which stored the king's
COURT (or   wardrobe.
Place)

WESTMINSTER A 'Minster' is a large church. This abbey church
             was situated to the west of the city. A charter of
             785 granted land to 'St. Peter and the needy
             people of God in Thorney in the terrible place
             which is called Westminster'.

WHITEFRIARS The Carmelite friars, who wore white habits, were
STREET   here from1241 until the Dissolution in the 16th
             century.

7 Tudor and Stuart London

In the church of St. Andrew Undershaft, in Leadenhall Street, is buried the topographer and historian of London, John Stow. On his tomb are carved books, bones and a spade – he was very interested in archaeology. The alabaster monument, erected by his wife, shows the antiquarian at work. The quill pen is replaced each year by the City Corporation. Stow was born in the parish of St. Michael Cornhill, the son and grandson of a tailor. Continuing the family tradition, John established himself as a master tailor, becoming a member of the Merchant Taylor's Company. *The Survey of London*, Stow's greatest work, was published in 1598, many years after his retirement. Antiquarianism was not lucrative. When in 1604 his poverty was brought to the attention of James I, the King authorized the chronicler to beg from the general public. This did little to help him, and he was still poor when he died the following year.

Edmond Howes, Stow's literary executor, describes the chronicler as 'tall of stature, lean of body and face, his eyes small and crystalline, of a pleasant and cheerful countenance . . . He always protested never to have written anything either for malice, fear or favour, nor to seek his own particular gain or vainglory; and that his only pains and care was to write truth.'

Stow senior had lived in Threadneedle Street close to a house of the London Austin Friars. (The present Austin Friar Square corresponds to the site of the cloisters.) When, in 1531–2, Thomas Cromwell built a house for himself in Throgmorton Street, on property acquired from the Friars, he expropriated part of the elder Stow's garden to the south, where there was a summer-house, in order to enlarge his own. The summer-house was transferred on rollers to Stow's sadly diminished garden. A mere tailor didn't like to argue with so great a man.

The days of the Austin Friars, and of all other monastic foundations, were numbered. Between 1536 and 1539 Cromwell carried through the Dissolution with a ruthlessness he had shown in

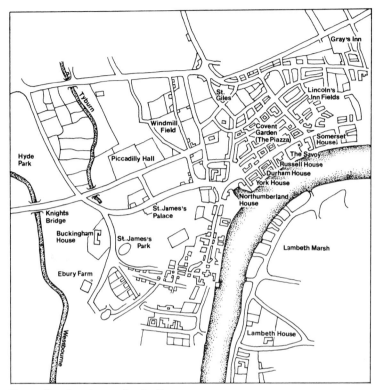

Expanding London under the Stuarts

extending his garden. For Londoners, disposed by their long tradition of anti-clericalism to weep few tears for the monks, the significance of the Dissolution was the new availability of land, especially outside the City walls. The City's expansion was now unobstructed. The Crown's greatest prize was the vast estates of Westminster Abbey, large tracts of which were eventually sold to wealthy laymen, such as the Duke of Bedford, who acquired the convent garden.

Stow's London, with its population in 1600 of around 200,000, seems small to us, but numbers were growing rapidly following the decline of the Black Death years, and the city was bursting at the seams. In 1580 the population of the East End was around 14,000. By 1630 the total would grow to something approaching 50,000. From his home in Leadenhall Street, Stow observed the early years of the East End's transformation. In his opinion it was 'no small

85

Stow's Monument in St. Andrew's Undershaft (Guildhall Library, City of London)

blemish for so famous a city to have so unsavery and unseemly an entry' as Whitechapel Road. He disliked the encroachments on the attractive common land called 'Mile End Waste' to the east of Aldgate. 'But this common field, I say, being sometime the beauty of this city on that part, is so encroached upon by building of filthy cottages that in some places it scarce remaineth a sufficient highway for the meeting of carriages and droves of cattle; much less is there any fair, pleasant or wholesome way for people to walk on foot . . .'

The guilds disliked the suburbs because the traders and craftsmen could now escape from their control. The mayor and aldermen, determined not to assume responsibility, wanted to arrest their growth. The Crown co-operated. In 1580 a royal proclamation

Whitehall as depicted on the bird's-eye view woodcut map attributed to Ralph Agas (the 'Agas' Map) c. 1562 (Guildhall Library, City of London)

prohibited new buildings within three miles of the city gates; but it was like Canute against the tide.

In the year of Stow's death, the villages to the east of the City were still scattered, the City of Westminster took up a narrow strip by the river. To the west, Covent Garden was undeveloped. In fact,

87

a Gate belonging to the Old palace of White Hall.

The Holbein Gate of the Palace of Whitehall. It was demolished in the 18th century. The surviving gate at St. James's Palace is similar. (Guildhall Library, City of London)

the entire West End had not yet been born – what is now Piccadilly was then countryside. At Charing Cross, where Dr Johnson would witness 'the full tide of human existence', there was the small village of Charing. Hampstead was a desolate moor, a haunt of criminals, surrounded by the Forest of Middlesex, traces of which may be seen at Kenwood. Cattle and sheep were pastured at Islington, then herded for slaughter at Smithfield. The corn for London's bread was ground in windmills at Finsbury, Islington, Lambeth and Greenwich, though the swelling number of mouths to feed meant that the city would draw an increasing amount of food from further afield.

Stow's expanding London contained landmarks, such as its gates, which Chaucer would have known, but St. Paul's had lost its spire, burned down in 1561, and it hadn't been replaced, as Hollar's 1647 panorama shows. There were new landmarks, notably the Royal Exchange (1568) between Cornhill and Threadneedle Street, with a hundred shops on the first floor above the colonnade, and the turreted Nonsuch House (No-other-such-house), prefabricated in Holland and erected on London Bridge in 1577. In the words of John Norden, who drew a famous map of Tudor London, the Bridge was 'comparable in itself to a little city'. Visscher's

Wenceslaus Hollar's 1647 panorama – the section showing St. Paul's (Guildhall Library, City of London)

panorama of 1616 makes this clear. Getting across it could be full of delays and even hazardous, for the narrowness of the road led to fatal traffic pile-ups. Not until the middle years of the 18th century were the houses removed and the road widened. Traffic regulation was a worsening problem in Tudor London. Stow remarked with older-generation cantakerousness that it was bound to exist 'for the world runs on wheels with many whose parents were glad to go on foot' – or maybe by boat. In his opinion carts and drays were a

Old St. Paul's in the early 17th century after the destruction of the spire (Guildhall Library, City of London)

Old London Bridge, from Visscher's 1616 panorama (Guildhall Library, City of London)

Somerset House on the Strand. The painting is attributed to Cornelius Bol (Dulwich Art Gallery)

plague. Current problems of urban congestion seem mild in comparison with what Thomas Dekker, the playwright, describes: 'At every corner men, women and children meet in such shoals that posts are set up of purpose to strengthen the houses lest with jostling one another they shoulder them down.'

As in Chaucer's day, the shops were stalls or sheds. Signs would swing to and fro in the wind. Though bricks had become popular, most of the buildings had wooden frames. Often the upper floors would jut out from the front, so that they overhung the street below. Thatched roofs had by now been totally replaced by tiles or lead, and the polluting smoke from the coal fires (which had superseded wood fires) was taken up through a chimney. Staple Inn in Holborn, built near the end of Elizabeth's reign, is a splendid and almost solitary example of a timbered Tudor building in London. Two others are Middle Temple Hall and the Queen's House in the Tower of London. Among the vanished Tudor glories were the Strand palaces, which by Elizabeth's reign were all occupied by courtiers – moving eastwards, York House, Durham House (on the present site of Shell-Mex House), Russell House, the Savoy, Somerset House, Arundel House and Leicester House. The aristocracy of this

91

Tudor Millionaire's Row wanted for little. A Venetian had observed about 1500 that London 'abounds with every article of luxury, as well as with the necessaries of life: but the most remarkable thing in London is the wonderful quantity of silver . . . In one single street, named the Strand, there are 52 goldsmith's shops . . .'

To a Scottish visitor, William Dunbar, London was 'the flower of cities all'. Yet the provision for sanitation and the disposal of refuse was no improvement on Chaucer's day. At night the stinking cesspits were emptied, as they would be for centuries hence. Rubbish was left in the streets to be picked up by the rakers. The gutters would still become blocked, the dirty water sometimes flooding the houses nearby. The poet Edmund Spenser might recall how he

Walk'd forth to ease my pain
Along the shore of silver-streaming Thames,
Whose rutty bank, the which his river hems
Was painted all with variable flowers . . .

but he might have been tempted at times to put a handkerchief to his nose. A German in London in 1598 commented that clothes washed in Thames water never lost the smell of mud and slime. The Walbrook and Fleet, and wells such as Clerkenwell, were also polluted and, according to Stow, the medieval ditch which surrounded the walls was 'of late neglected and forced either to a very narrow, and the same a filthy channel, or altogether stopped up for gardens planted and houses built thereon . . .'

Stow further informs us that Houndsditch was so called since it served as a depository for large numbers of dead dogs. Men in authority wished to improve the unpalatable. Periodically, sections of the ditch were cleaned – for example in 1519, between Aldgate and the Tower: 'The chief ditcher had by the day seven pence, the second ditcher six pence, the other ditchers five pence. And every vagabond (and so they were termed) one penny the day, meat and drink, at the charge of the city. £93.3s.4d' (Stow).

The results of these operations were temporary. In 1595 the ditch was cleared between Bishopsgate and Moorgate 'but filling again very fast'. The City wall, or at least the large section between Aldersgate and Aldgate, was in a better state, owing to a durable effort by several wealthy guilds in 1476–7.

The pressure on space inside the walls fostered the growth of the very different suburbs to east and west, a development which – in spite of a system of fines and licences introduced by James I – the city and the Crown failed to arrest; indeed, James I and Charles I were only too pleased to accept the fines.

Whitehall, and later St. James's, to which Charles II moved, drew the rich and fashionable to the west. Plagues, traffic congestion and pollution all encouraged the migration. Plague was inseparable from insanitary conditions. Traffic congestion was caused by the increasing number of hackney coaches and sedan chairs, a worrying trend for the watermen, who had ferried the citizens for centuries. (Their days were numbered, but many watermen's steps survive, such as Old Barge House Stairs on the south bank, near Blackfriars Bridge).

Pollution was made worse by the growth of small industries in the City and its eastern environs. John Evelyn would write of the undesirable effects of the burning of sea-coal. In *Fumifugium* or *The Smoake of London Dissipated* (1661) he wrote that the pea-soup fogs made it impossible to grow anemones without 'extraordinary artifice'. 'It is this horrid smoake which obscures our churches, and makes our Palaces look old, which fouls our clothes, and corrupts the Waters . . . It is this which scatters and strews about those black and smutty Atomes upon all things where it comes, insinuating itself into our very secret cabinets, and most precious Repositories.'

Evelyn observed that even Whitehall and Westminster were often filled with smoke from nearby brew-houses. The 'extraordinary stench' of fog over St. Paul's was particularly distressing. The fog was not only bad for health; it also undermined law and order, since thieves could operate with impunity. The fog was sometimes so thick over the river that drums were used to guide the watermen towards the shore. From time immemorial the greater part of London's water supply had been drawn from the Thames and distributed in buckets by the water carriers, but the purity of the product would not have satisfied us. Pollution was equally a problem in the wells from which water was also drawn. Conduits supplied by outlying springs were the chief source of fresh water, but this system (which predated Chaucer) was overstretched, with fewer than twenty conduit heads to supply a booming population. A gentleman from Bath named Edmund Colthurst suggested that a cleaner supply might be tapped from spring water in Hertfordshire, then distributed by pipes to the houses. Colthurst proposed to divert the waters into a new river which he would lead into a reservoir to the north of the city. Brilliant ideas require men possessing influence and capital to put them into operation. Colthurst's scheme was taken up by the wealthy goldsmith, Hugh Myddleton.

Unfortunately, work on the river was brought to a halt by the objections of the affected landowners. It was now that King James played an essential part by agreeing to pay for half the cost of the venture in return for a half share in its future profits. The involvement of the King enabled the work to progress more smoothly. In 1618 the New River was supplemented by water drawn from the River Lea. From the reservoir, which was constructed in Clerkenwell, water flowed out in pipes to those prepared to pay the rent. The new supply fostered the growth of the northern suburbs, something which the Stuart government, like its predecessor, wanted to prevent. The New River, which is no longer used as a source of supply, now terminates at the Stoke Newington Waterworks. The reservoir in Clerkenwell is the site of the headquarters of the Metropolitan Water Board.

The growing suburbs in the west were of the tasteful kind. The one closest to the city was Lincoln's Inn Fields. By 1642, when civil war interrupted the scheme, most of the south and west sides were lined with houses. Back in 1617 James had asked Inigo Jones, his surveyor-general, to turn three meadows into a place of 'public health and pleasure'. The son of a Smithfield clothworker, Inigo had established his reputation as a designer of sets for masques, the splendid court entertainments much beloved by King James. Later, his travels in Italy had brought him under the classical influence of Palladio. It was in this Palladian style, which recalls the austere and formal grandeur of the public buildings of Greece and Rome, that Inigo Jones built the Queen's House for Anne of Denmark in the grounds of Greenwich Palace. It now forms the central part of the Maritime Museum. Between 1619 and 1622 he built the Banqueting House in Whitehall, intended as part of a wholesale reconstruction of the palace, of which the plans still survive. The sheer expense prevented the enterprise. In Lincoln's Inn Fields the resident lawyers proved the obstruction, and the scheme didn't get started till 1629.

In 1632 Francis Russell, fourth Earl of Bedford, was allowed to develop Covent (i.e. Convent) Garden, an area which had originally been a kitchen garden belonging to the monks of Westminster. Following the Dissolution, the Crown sold it to John Russell, first Earl of Bedford. When discussing the construction of a proposed church with Inigo Jones, the fourth Earl, a low churchman who liked to save money, said that he wanted something like a barn. Inigo, who himself wanted his buildings to be 'masculine, solid, simple', told him that he would have the handsomest barn in England for £5,000. The church of St. Paul's

Covent Garden and Bedford House as depicted on Wenceslaus Hollar's bird's-eye view of 1658 (Guildhall Library, City of London)

formed the western side of the square. Rebuilt in the original style after a fire in 1795, it is still there today – 'the actors' church'. The impressive portico on the east was never used because the altar was moved to this end, probably on the orders of Archbishop Laud. On the piazza's northern and eastern sides were splendid houses of red brick with their front doors opening out on to vaulted arcades. Bedford Chambers, built in the last century, recall their appearance. To the south was the garden wall of Bedford House. A market, modest at first, soon started; this lined the pockets of the fifth Earl, but when it took over the piazza the genteel residents, not liking the hubbub, moved out – maybe to Leicester Square, built up in the 1670s, or maybe further west. Around Covent Garden were built streets of slightly inferior houses, though all showing the influence of Inigo Jones: James Street, Russell Street and Henrietta Street (named after Henrietta Maria, the wife of Charles I).

Not all the aristocratic developers of the day were so successful as the fourth Earl of Bedford – the Earl of Leicester, for example, who had built a house along one side of Leicester Fields, was not granted permission to build an estate. This relieved the countrymen who had been alarmed by the plans – the unpopular developer is an old

The 2 of May, 1643 y Croße in Cheapeside was pulled downe a Troope of Horse & 2 Companies of foote wayted to garde it & at y fall of y tope Croße dromes beat trupets blew & multitudes of Capes wayre throwne in y Ayre & a greate Shoute of People with ioy; y 2 of May the Almana ke sayeth, was y invention of the Croße, & 6 day at night was the Leaden Popes burnt in the pla ce where it ßood with ringinge of Bells & a greate Acclamation & no hurt done in all these actions.

10 of May the Boocke of Spartes vpon the Lords day was burnt by the Hangman in the place where the Croße ßoode, & at Exchange

Puritan Fervour – the Eleanor Cross in Cheapside is pulled down in 1643. The etching is by Wenceslaus Hollar (Guildhall Library, City of London)

phenomenon. In the end the developers had their way. As some kind of memorial to the countrymen, even today Leicester Square preserves the irregular shape of a field.

One major project originated with a tailor, a certain Robert Baker, who built a house called Piccadilly Hall, at the east end of what became Piccadilly. Baker's fortune partly derived from the making of stiff collars called pickadils – hence the name.

Nothing less than the Civil War was required to bring the remarkable spate of building to a temporary halt. London was the Puritans' trump card – a vital source of wealth and manpower. New fortifications were built – twenty-four forts and eighteen miles of earthworks. A fragment of an Eleanor Cross in the Museum of London bears witness to Puritan enthusiasm. The destruction was witnessed by John Evelyn. 'May 2nd being at Lond: I saw the furious and rabid Mobile throw down, and breake to pieces, the crossse in Cheap-side . . . To that ungoverned Exorbitance were things come, thro' the malice, and mistaken zeale of the fanatic Magistrats, dipt in the Rebellion.' By 1660 the citizens had had enough of Puritan intolerance – the fact that Oliver Cromwell was married to the daughter of a London merchant did nothing to redeem his rule – and they welcomed Charles II. The son of the Puritan fanatic 'Praise God' Barebones was the worldly Dr. Nicholas Barbon, a property developer (numbers 36–43 Bedford Row are some of his surviving houses) and the founder of London's first fire insurance company (the Phoenix) formed a few years after the greatest disaster in its history.

London had barely recovered from its worst plague since the Black Death when, in the early autumn of 1666, a raging fire reduced much of it to a pile of rubble. The unplanned medieval city, with its narrow cobbled streets and overhanging timbered dwellings, then underwent a change of face. To some extent at least, the fire marks the end of the old city and the beginning of the new. The new city, more hygenic than the old, would be virtually free of the plague. Of course, the slums didn't magically disappear. The uninviting parish of St. Giles-in-the-Fields where the plague of 1665 broke out would become Tom-All-Alone's in Dickens's *Bleak House*. 'It is a moot point whether Tom-All-Alone's be uglier by day or by night.' Now it is New Oxford Street – hardly beautiful, but certainly an improvement.

Christopher Wren, to whom the disaster was a golden opportunity, had been born in Wiltshire, the son of a rector. His grandfather had been a London mercer. Within a few days of the fire being put out, this young and fertile genius, already the country's foremost astronomer, proposed a scheme for the new city. This would have erased the cramped streets of the medieval lay-out, replacing it with a plan both grand and spacious. It was the product

St. Mary-le-Bow   St.Bride   St.Magnus the Martyr

Three contrasting Wren spires

of an astronomer's ordered, sweeping vision. But people returned
to their former plots, which only alternative plots would have
persuaded them to yield. Widespread exchanges would have
required an exhaustive survey of land-ownership in the burnt area
of London. Such a survey proved impossible to carry out. So Wren's
dream went unrealized, though it helped to win him the post of
surveyor-general, the key architectural post which Inigo Jones had
held before him.

The main feature of old London was its churches, and a church-building programme was the new surveyor-general's chief task. Money for this, as for all other public projects, was raised by a tax of three shillings on every ton of coal entering the Port of London. Although eighty-seven of the hundred and seven city churches (this figure includes the ten in the City Without the Wall) had been destroyed, the decision was made to rebuild only fifty-one. Had Wren's plan been adopted, these churches would have been an integral part of the general plan. As it was, Wren had to fit them into spaces that were sometimes small and inconveniently shaped, a fact which partly explains the absence of chancels. Wren's interiors were marked by towering Corinthian pillars, generally supporting barrel-vaulted roofs, while galleries above the side aisles formed by the pillars provided extra seating space for the congregation. Of course, the scheme has many variations; no two churches are exactly alike. Three of the finest are St. Mary-le-Bow, St. Bride and St. Magnus the Martyr. The old churches had been mostly small-towered, and usually without spires. London's skyline was marvellously transformed by Wren's tall steeples, masterpieces of classical design. Victorian insensitivity, a declining resident population and Germany's bombs in the Second World War have all contributed to the disappearance of a number of the city churches, including many of Wren's. Thirty-nine now remain, restored in the post-war years.

The restoration of St. Paul's had been in slow progress – with an interruption during Puritan rule – for some time. John Evelyn and Christopher Wren were both members of a commission which had been inspecting the cathedral a few days before the Fire. 'We had in mind to build it with a noble cupola' reported Evelyn. In 1670 Wren submitted drawings for an entirely new St. Paul's. Like his plan for the city, the so-called 'New Model' was rejected. Three years later, Wren produced another plan, of which a wooden model was constructed, still to be seen at St. Paul's. This was also rejected. Wren produced his third scheme, the 'nightmare' design, which had a spire and funnel-shaped dome. This was accepted. In fact, the cathedral which evolved was like the 'Great Model', the second plan.

St. Paul's is a memorial not only to Wren's architectural genius but also to the work of some of the best craftsmen and artists of the day. Four examples will suffice: the choir-stalls and bishop's throne of Grinling Gibbons, the master wood-carver; the splendid ironwork of Jean Tijou, the finest smith of the age, which may be seen in the dean's staircase and in the gates leading to the apse; the marble font of Francis Bird, who also carved the *Conversion of St. Paul* in the west pediment; finally, the eight huge scenes of Sir

James Thornhill which adorn the dome. The cathedral took thirty-five years to build. There is a tradition that Wren watched the building from a house on the south side of the river (No. 49 Cardinal Cap Alley, which alley is exactly focused on St. Paul's). In 1710 Wren's son placed the final stone on the lantern that crowns the dome. In his declining years Sir Christopher was brought each year from Hampton to survey his greatest work. He died in the Old Court House, within a stone's throw of the palace, at the ripe age of 91. 'Lector, si monumentum requiris, circumspice,' says the tablet over his tombstone in the crypt of St. Paul's. 'Reader, if you seek a memorial, look around.'

Further Reading

A Survey of London   John Stow (Dent, Everyman)

Elizabethan London   M. R. Holmes (Cassell, 1969)

Tudor London   Philippa Glanville (Museum of London, 1980)

The Growth of Stuart London   N. G. Brett-James (Allen and Unwin, 1935)

London and the Outbreak of the Puritan Revolution   Valerie Pearl (OUP, 1961)

The Rebuilding of London after the Great Fire   T. F. Reddaway (Arnold, 1951)

Life in Stuart London   Peggy Miller (Methuen, 1977)

The Making of the Metropolis: London 1500–1700   Ed. A. L. Beier and Roger Finlay (Longman, 1986)

8 Historic London (3)

Richmond Palace
(formerly the Palace of Shene),
Richmond Green, near Richmond Bridge

The first king to occupy the palace of Shene was Henry I in 1125. It was a favourite residence of Richard II and his wife, Anne of Bohemia. After Anne's death in 1394, Richard ordered its demolition. A new palace was destroyed by fire in 1499. Henry VII built a third palace on the site, naming it Richmond in honour of his title of Earl of Richmond (in Yorkshire). Both he and Elizabeth I died here. The GATEWAY and WARDROBE survive.

The Chapel of the Savoy, Savoy Street
(off the Strand)

The original Savoy Palace, belonging to the hated John of Gaunt, was burned down by the peasants in 1381. Henry VII rebuilt it as a hospital, but only the chapel has survived.

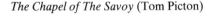

The Chapel of The Savoy (Tom Picton)

The entrance courtyard of Fulham Palace (Tom Picton)

Fulham Palace, near Putney Bridge

The residence of the Bishops of London for centuries. The entrance courtyard, the oldest surviving part of the building, was built by Bishop FitzJames in the reign of Henry VII. The thirty-seven acres of beautiful grounds are adjoined by Bishop's Park, which borders the Thames.

St. James's Palace showing Henry VIII's Gatehouse (Guildhall Library, City of London)

St. James's Palace and Park

St. James's Palace occupies the site of a medieval hospital dedicated to St. James The Less. Henry VIII acquired the hospital and its grounds in 1531 and built a palace, of which the **Gatehouse**, the **Old Presence Chamber** and the **Chapel Royal** survive. Charles II employed Sir Christopher Wren to provide state apartments overlooking the park.

After the burning down of Whitehall in 1698, St. James's Palace became the sovereign's official London residence. Even today the British court is known officially as the Court of St. James's, and the sovereign is proclaimed from the balcony in **Friary Court**. The palace was restored by John Nash.

Don't forget to admire the 16th-century gatehouse facing St. James's Street. Over the doors are the carved initials of Henry VIII and Anne Boleyn.

A walled Park was laid out by Henry VIII. Charles I walked across it on his way to the scaffold in Whitehall. After the restoration a 'canal' was made from the scattered ponds by the great Le Nôtre (of Versailles fame), and in 1827–9 John Nash landscaped the park and lake we see today. Look out for the pelicans, which are descended from a brace given by the Russian ambassador to Charles II.

The **Chapel Royal** was built for Henry VIII. The ceiling (1540) was probably designed by Holbein. It has long enjoyed a reputation for fine music; Orlando Gibbons and Henry Purcell were among its early organists. The resident choir, the private choir of the sovereign, is composed of six 'gentlemen' and ten boys.

Several royal marriages have taken place here, including those of Queen Victoria (1840) and George V (1893).

Hampton Court Palace

Hampton Court Palace was begun in 1514 by Cardinal Wolsey. It was not only more splendid but also, owing to its excellent drainage system and clean water supply, far healthier than the royal palaces. In 1529 all the Cardinal's lands and goods were declared forfeit to the King. Henry eagerly took over both York Place, which he renamed Whitehall Palace, and Hampton Court, where he added the Great Hall, with its hammer-beam roof and walls hung with Brussels tapestries, and the fan-vaulted wooden ceiling in the Chapel Royal.

By the time of William III (1688–1702) the Tudor palace seemed out of date and inconvenient. Christopher Wren was employed by the King to plan a new palace. One scheme would have entailed the destruction of all the Tudor buildings except the Great Hall. The adopted scheme preserved the Base Court and the Clock Court, but the third courtyard, round which the state apartments were grouped, was demolished to make way for the Fountain Court and the building of classical style which we see today. After the death of George II in 1760, the palace ceased to be a royal residence.

Enter the **Outer Green Court** through the **Trophy Gates**, built in the reign of George II. The river is to your right. The west side of the palace is ahead. The moat in front is crossed by a bridge built by Henry VIII, who added wings at either end of the west front. Between them is the entrance of Wolsey's house, and in the middle is his **Great Gatehouse**.

It was usual for Tudor palaces to be built around three courtyards. Pass through to the **Base Court**, the first of them. **Anne**

EVERYBODY'S HISTORIC LONDON

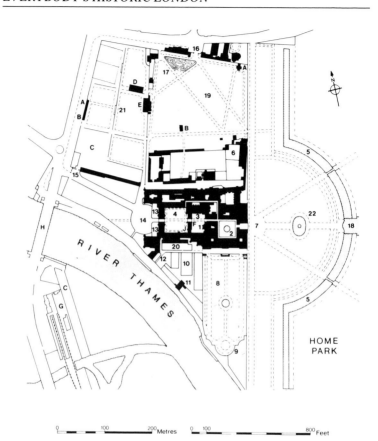

A B C D E F G H J
A Ladies' Lavatories
B Gentlemen's Lavatories
C Car Park
D Cafeteria
E Restaurant
F Shop
G Hampton Court Railway Station
H Hampton Court Bridge
J Ticket Office

1 Entrance to State Apartments and Renaissance
  Picture Gallery
2 Fountain Court
3 Clock Court
4 Base Court
5 Canal

6 Tennis Court
7 East Front
8 Privy Garden
9 Tijou Screen
10 Pond Garden
11 Banqueting House
12 Great Vine
13 Moat
14 West Front
15 Main Entrance (Trophy Gates)
16 Lion Gates
17 Maze
18 Long Water
19 Wilderness
20 Lower Orangery (Mantegna Gallery)
21 Tiltyard Gardens
22 Fountain Garden

A plan of Hampton Court Palace and grounds (Controller of Her Majesty's
Stationery Office)

The main entrance front of Wolsey's house. His Great Gatehouse in the centre (Guildhall Library, City of London)

Boleyn's Gateway leads to the **Clock Court**, the main courtyard of Wolsey's house. On the left is Henry VIII's **Great Hall**.

Find time to study the **Astronomical Clock**, made for Henry VIII. This shows the hour, the month, the day of the month and the phrases of the moon. Note that the sun revolves around the earth – the clock was constructed before Copernicus and Galileo.

Pass through the **George II Gateway** to the **Fountain Court**, and from here to the **Broad Walk**. In front is the **Great Fountain Garden**, a semicircle of grass and flower-beds crossed by three radiating avenues of trees and bounded by a canal. Beyond the canal is **Home Park**, which is bisected by the **Long Water**, at right angles to the Broad Walk. The Long Water was constructed in Charles II's reign. In Home Park William III had his fatal hunting accident when his horse put a foot in a mole-hole, which is why the Jacobites toasted 'the little gentleman in black velvet'. From here is the best view of the section of the palace which was built for William and Mary by Christopher Wren.

If you turn to the right along Broad Walk, you come to a gateway which opens onto the terrace along the south side of the Wren building. Steps descend to the **Privy Garden**, at the far end of which is a magnificent wrought-iron screen designed by Jean Tijou. Other gardens include the **Pond Garden**, a sunk garden laid out by Henry VIII. Beyond is the **Great Vine**, planted in 1769, which produces a fine annual corp of black grapes. To the right is the **Lower Orangery**. Overlooking the river is William III's **Banqueting House**.

If you turn to the left along Broad Walk, you will come to the entrance to the **Tennis Court** (for real tennis – not the Wimbledon variety!) built by William III on the site of Henry VIII's court; and then to the **Wilderness,** the **Maze**, laid out in the reign of Queen Anne, and the **Lion Gates**. West of the Wilderness are the **Tiltyard Gardens** on the site of the Tiltyard where Henry VIII held his jousts.

On the opposite side of Hampton Court Road is **Bushy Park** (used by Henry VIII as a royal hunting preserve). The **Chestnut Avenue** in Bushy Park was planned to form the main approach to the completely rebuilt palace which never materialized.

The Royal Exchange

The Royal Exchange was founded in 1568 by Sir Thomas Gresham, goldsmith, banker and Merchant Adventurer. The Adventurers were mainly concerned with the export of cloth, which had replaced wool as the chief export. In 1565, it amounted to over 78 per cent of the total value of exports, four-fifths of which were handled by the

The First Royal Exchange. The etching is by Wenceslaus Hollar (Guildhall Library, City of London)

City. Modelled on the Bourse at Antwerp, the Royal Exchange was upstairs a shopping arcade, known as the Pawn, and, in the covered walk and central quadrangle below, a meeting-place for merchants, who had been used to doing their business in the nave of St. Paul's (Paul's Walk).

In spite of Gresham's Bourse, London didn't altogether acquire Antwerp's mantle when 'the warehouse of all Christendom' went into sharp decline. Virtually unrivalled commercial supremacy wasn't achieved till the 18th century. Meanwhile, the Royal Exchange declined in importance, being effectively replaced by the Stock Exchange. The first Stock Exchange building was erected in 1773 at the corner of Threadneedle Street and Sweetings Alley. For a long while previously the brokers had met in coffee houses in the vicinity of the Royal Exchange. Lloyds also had a coffee-house origin. Following the destruction of the first Exchange in the Great Fire, businessmen interested in marine insurance came to gather in Edward Lloyd's coffee house in Tower Street.

The Gresham family crest was a grasshopper, sign of his goldsmith's shop in Lombard Street. A grasshopper-vane, a survival from the original exchange, may be seen on the Victorian Royal Exchange (the third) of our own day.

The Theatre, Shakespeare and the Borough

In the early days of the London theatre, companies of strolling players presented their dramas in the courtyards of inns. At some of them, such as the Bull in Bishopsgate, performances were frequent. The enthusiasm was shared by the queen, though not by the mayor and corporation. 'The cause of plague is sin, and the cause of sin is plays: therefore the causes of plague are plays' was one form of reasoning. The masterpieces of Marlowe and Shakespeare were dismissed along with bear-baiting, cock-fighting and other disreputable amusements which brought together the common herd; indeed, the same premises were often used. A Puritan warned that actors are 'masters of vice, teachers of wantonness, spurs to impurity, and sons of idleness'. In 1575 they were expelled from the city. The lack of suitable inns on the outskirts accounts for the purpose-built theatres, built in a style resembling the inn courtyards. The first was the Theatre in Finsbury Fields, whose site is marked by a plaque in Curtain Road, which runs parallel to

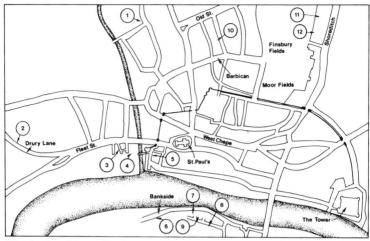

Elizabethan Theatreland

1. Red Bull	5. Blackfriars	9. Rose
2. Cockpit	6. Swan	10. Fortune
3. Whitefriars	7. Hope	11. The Theatre
4. Salisbury Court	8. Globe	12. Curtain

Shoreditch High Street. Its builder was James Burbage, the shrewd businessman father of the famous actor, Richard. The raw materials of the Theatre were later ferried across the Thames to build the Globe in Southwark, the most celebrated of the early theatres, where Shakespeare's tragedies were first performed.

Stow's London is the city described in the bard's masterpieces. Young Will, recently burdened by family responsibilities, set out from Stratford to London in about 1585. By 1594 he was a leading member of the Lord Chamberlain's Men, one of the actors' companies, working at the Theatre with Richard Burbage. Later he crossed the Thames and became a shareholder in that immensely profitable undertaking, the Globe Theatre. Its main rival was the Rose (the Lord Admiral's Men) on the corner of Rose Alley and Maid Lane.

To his contemporaries, Shakespeare was only one of a number of stars. Surrounding him were playwrights of remarkable gifts – Marlowe, Jonson (whose *Bartholomew Fair* gives the best theatrical portrait of contemporary London), Webster, Greene, Beaumont, Fletcher . . . When not acting or writing, these sparkling personalities would assemble in certain London taverns such as the Mermaid in Cheapside and the George and the Anchor in Southwark. (The two Southwark inns survive, though Shakespeare didn't know the present buildings, which date from the 17th century). Thomas Fuller, looking back some years later, compared Jonson to a great Spanish galleon and Shakespeare to the smaller and more mobile English man-of-war. Jonson was 'far higher in learning but solid and slow in his performances while Shakespeare, lesser in bulk but light in sailing, could turn with all tides, tack about, take advantage of all winds by the quickness of his wit and invention'. To our loss there was no Tudor equivalent of Boswell. The lives of the Tudor dramatists were intensely productive, though often pitifully short. Marlowe was killed in a tavern duel at the age of twenty-nine. Beaumont and Greene died in their early thirties.

On the wall of **Courage's Brewery** (which was owned in the 18th century by Henry Thrale, Dr Johnson's friend) is a plaque marking the site of the **Globe Theatre**, 'this wooden O', where fifteen of Shakespeare's plays were produced. The first Globe was built by Richard and Cuthbert Burbage with the timber of the Theatre, which had been erected by their father in 1576. It was burned down in 1613, and its replacement was demolished in 1644. (The latest Globe, a reconstruction of the original, was opened in 1996.) Other theatres built on Bankside were the Rose, the Hope and the Swan. Being within the Liberty of the Clink (see 'The Borough and Southwark Cathedral), they were immune to the City's puritanical jurisdiction.

The **Shakespeare Globe Museum**, occupying a 19th-century warehouse, has a permanent exhibition relating a Elizabethan theatre and also a model of a frost fair.

Southwark Cathedral contains a memorial to Shakespeare, 'for

A model of The Globe Theatre (Guildhall Library, City of London)

Sir Paul Pindar's house in Bishopsgate photographed in 1890 (Guildhall Library, City of London)

Three Pre-Great Fire Houses

Pre-Great Fire Houses are very rare in London – don't be misled by Liberty's (1923)! – which is why we should make a fuss of them! One Jacobean example is at No. 17 Fleet Street, leading to the Inner Temple. On the first floor, over the gateway, is a chamber known as **Prince Henry's Room**, named after the subject of the decorated ceiling, the popular elder son of James I. **Cloth Fair**, north of the church of St. Bartholomew the Great, marks the site once occupied

Ham House – country home of a Jacobean courtier (Tom Picton)

by the booths of drapers and clothiers, including at one time the father of Inigo Jones. Don't miss the carefully preserved **Merchant's House** at No. 41 (*c*. 1640). For my third choice, take a bus to South Kensington where, in the Victoria and Albert Museum, part of **Sir Paul Pindar's Jacobean House**, which used to stand in Bishopsgate, may be seen.

Ham House,* Richmond (on the Petersham Road)

Ham House was built in 1610 by a courtier of James 1, through the furnishings mostly date from the later part of the century. Here we find paintings by Constable, Kneller and Reynolds, and a portrait of Elizabeth 1 by Nicholas Hilliard, the celebrated miniaturist.

* For a full account of this stately home, and of stately homes generally, see *Life in the English Country House* by Mark Girouard (Yale University Press, 1978, also in Penguin).

The Banqueting House, Whitehall and Horse Guards Parade

The Palladian Banqueting House was built by Inigo Jones between 1619 and 1622, and formed part of the Palace of Whitehall, once York Place, the London residence of the Archbishop of York. It is possible that Charles I passed through one of the windows at the north end of the hall to the black-draped scaffold erected in the roadway. However, he may have passed to the scaffold through a window in a northern annexe that no longer exists.

Spot the weathercock which, it is said, James II installed to determine whether the wind would help or hinder William of Orange's invasion in 1688. Unfortunately for Catholic James, it proved a 'Protestant wind'.

The Queen's House, Greenwich (now part of the National Maritime Museum)

Begun for Anne of Denmark, the consort of James I, and designed by Inigo Jones, this is the first example in England of the Palladian style. (After Palladio, an Italian architect who set down rules of classic proportion, such as the double cube.) The insistence on complete symmetry took English masons by surprise. Previously used to being inventive, they were told by Inigo to follow his drawings with absolute precision. The Queen's House was completed for Henrietta Maria, the consort of Charles I, though later on (1661) it was changed from an H-shape into the square we see today. The 'House of Delight', as Henrietta Maria called it, is now connected by colonnades to east and west wings of the early 19th century.

The Queen's House, Greenwich – an example of Palladian architecture by Inigo Jones (Guildhall Library, City of London)

The Queen's Chapel
Marlborough Road, off the Mall

Designed by Inigo Jones in the Palladian style, it was begun for the Roman Catholic Infanta Maria of Spain, whom the future Charles I (1625–49) made a famous bid to marry, and, like the Queen's House, completed for the French princess, Henrietta Maria, another Catholic, whom he did marry.

KEW PALACE.

Kew Palace – a favourite retreat of the Hanoverians (Guildhall Library, City of London)

Kew Palace

Built in 1631 by the son of a Dutch refugee, this red brick, typically Dutch style residence was later a favoured Hanoverian retreat. Fanny Burney who was a novelist, diarist and for a time Mistress of the Robes to Queen Charlotte, wife of George III, recorded on 8 August 1786 that they 'came, as usual on every alternate Tuesday, to Kew'. For the gardens we must thank Princess Augusta, the mother of George III, who employed Sir William Chambers (of Somerset House fame) to design some buildings, which include the pagoda and the orangery. The Queen's cottage (the Queen in this case was Caroline, wife of George II) is south of the lake and close to Old Deer Park.

St. Giles Rookery and the Plague (1665)*

The worst plague since the Black Death broke out in the neighbourhood of our New Oxford Street. Then it was the uninviting parish of St. Giles-in-the-Fields, or St. Giles Rookery, which remained a slum area until the early 20th century. In *Bleak House* Dickens called it Tom-All-Alone's. 'It is a moot point whether Tom-All-Alone's be uglier by day or by night; but on the argument that the more that is seen of it the more shocking it must be, and that no part of it left to the imagination is at all likely to be made so bad as the reality, day carries it.'

There was a solitary victim in February. The blighted family's house, wooden and dilapidated like the others in the area, was marked with a red cross on the door and the words 'Lord have mercy upon us' written up. The prayer was not a meaningless formula for it was feared by many that plague was God's punishment for sinfulness. Like Sodom and Gomorrah, London was receiving its just desserts.

At the end of April, Samuel Pepys was noting a lively apprehension in the city: 'Great fears of the sickness here in the city, it being said that 2 or 3 houses are already shut up. God preserve us all!'. The plague had now spread to the parish of St. Clement Danes, from where it moved by way of Holborn and Chancery Lane to the Strand. William Boghurst, a conscientious and observant doctor in St. Giles-in-the-Fields, compiled a list of symptoms which ranged from swellings and spots to delirium and despair. Neither Boghurst nor anyone else guessed the true cause of the plague.

Before the end of June the wealthy, including the entire court, poured out of London. 'To the Cross Keys at Cripplegate', wrote Pepys on 21 June, 'where I find all the towne almost going out of towne, the coaches and waggons being all full of people going into the country.' Never had so many regulations been issued in so short a space of time: schools must close; lodgers, pedlars and minstrels must quit the city; domestic animals – conveyors of infection, so it was thought – must be slaughtered. (Unfortunately, the destruction of the cats could only lead to an increase in the real culprits, the black rats which carried the fleas). All burials must take place before sunrise or after sunset. At the appropriate times the death carts came rattling down the cobbled streets, while the lugubrious

* The standard account is W. G. Bell, *The Great Plague in London in 1665* (The Bodley Head, 1924) republished as *The Great Plague of London* (Bracken Books, 1994).

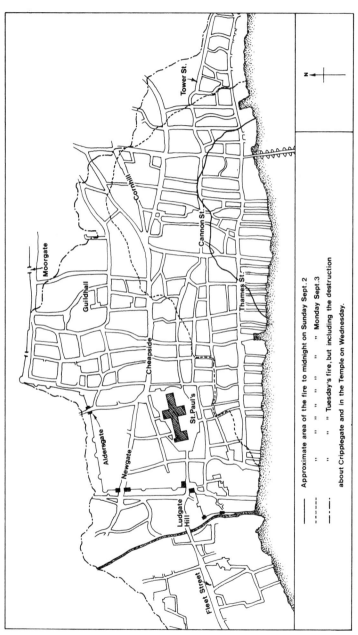

Approximate area of the fire to midnight on Sunday Sept. 2
" " " " " " " Monday Sept.3
" " " Tuesday's fire, but including the destruction
about Cripplegate and in the Temple on Wednesday.

The Extent of The Great Fire 1666

cries of 'Bring out your dead!' filled the air. Pits were dug in the open country to accommodate the corpses. In spite of the regulations, the plague spread to Westminster and to Southwark, claiming 6,000 victims in July. In the first week of August there were 4,000 deaths, and this figure continued to rise relentlessly. It was 7,500 deaths for the fourth week, 8,000 for the first week in September. At this desperate juncture fires were lit in the streets. The aim of the operation was to purify the air, but disaster ensued when a rainstorm turned the flames into choking fumes, which in the space of a night dispatched 4,000 sufferers. At about this time it appears that the plague took on the pneumonic form. The illness was now often briefer – the patients dying in under two days while showing signs of mental disorder.

'But Lord!' wrote Pepys in mid-September. 'What a sad time it is to see no boats upon the river; and grass grows up and down White Hall Court, and nobody put poor wretches in the streets!' No longer were affected families prepared to live as excluded lepers. Omnipresent death resulted in a carelessness and a wilful defiance of regulations – much to Samuel Pepys's alarm: 'There is now no observation of shutting-up of houses infected, to be sure we do converse and meet with people that have the plague upon them.' Yet Pepys survived, though he lost his doctor, and also his waiter at the Angel tavern.

In October there came an improvement. By the last week deaths were down to 1,421, though in the region of the Tower, where Pepys lived, the plague continued to rage. It had travelled across the City from St. Giles-in-the-Fields in the west to Stepney in the east. Not until December did the rich consider it safe to return.

The Monument and the Fire*

Wren's Monument, 202 feet high, was erected during 1671–77 to commemorate the Great Fire, which broke out, we are supposed to believe, exactly 202 feet away in Pudding Lane. The relief portrays Charles II and James Duke of York rallying the afflicted city.

Pudding Lane was a short distance from the northern shore of the Thames, very close to London Bridge. It was a typical London street:

* The standard account is W. G. Bell, *The Great Fire in London in 1666* (The Bodley Head, 1923) republished as *The Great Fire of London* (Bracken Books, 1994).

cobbled, narrow, with the overhanging upper stories of the timbered hovels on either side of it not far from touching in the middle. A chance combination of circumstances – the recent dry weather, the direction of the wind, the highly inflammable substances stored in the warehouses on the north bank – turned a local mishap into a major disaster.

In the early hours of Sunday 2 September, a spark from the fire in Thomas Farynor's bakehouse was blown by a strong North-east wind to the Star inn in Fish Street Hill, which ran parallel with Pudding Lane. Here the bales of hay and straw which filled the yard and outhouses guaranteed a conflagration which spread quickly to the foot of London Bridge. The roaring flames encircled the tower of the church of St. Magnus the Martyr, then, stoked by various substances inside the warehouses, travelled westward along the river bank as far as Baynard's Castle. Later, houses at the north end of the bridge succumbed. Here a fire-break – left on purpose after a fire in 1633 – stopped the conflagration from spreading to Southwark.

Mayor Bludworth, who was nominally in charge of the fire-fighting operation, refused to order the systematic destruction of property in the path of the fire. He underestimated the danger. 'A chambermaid could piss it out,' he is supposed to have said. Given Bludworth's reluctance to take the bold step of destroying property, the conflagration had to be fought by conventional means, which were proving ineffective. The fire-fighters were not helped by the tide of refugees constantly pushing past them. Countrymen, prompted by a mixture of altruism and financial calculation, poured into the city to assist their flight; a cart had suddenly become a valuable commodity. In the confusion one of the best hand-operated pumping-engines was forced into the river. There was a serious problem of water supply; the conduits ran too slowly, the level in the wells was too low, while the supplies from the New River were running to waste since the pipes had already been cut in various places. Passing up buckets from the Thames was a painfully slow process.

Samuel Pepys showed extraordinary energy during the crisis. He rushed to Whitehall, where he appeared before Charles and his brother, James Duke of York. Following Pepys's advice, the king ordered that Bludworth should be found and commanded to 'spare no houses but to pull down before the fire every way'. However, when the mayor cautiously started upon the work of demolition, the fire constantly caught up with him – this was in spite of the assistance of soldiers sent by the Duke of York. He at last gave up and went home. On Monday York was to be given control of the fire-fighting operations.

On Sunday evening Pepys took to a boat. The fire was now moving from the river towards the centre of the city. His diarist's eye was riveted by the scene ashore. 'We stayed till, it being darkish, we saw the fire as only one entire arch of fire from this to the other side of the bridge, and in a bow up the hill for an arch of about a mile long. It made me weep to see it.' By nightfall the fire was blazing along half a mile of the river bank on both sides of London Bridge, and the city centre was almost within its grip. On Monday it continued unabated. By the evening the ancient halls of the livery companies were collapsing, while Gresham's Royal Exchange stood in imminent danger. 'London was, but is no more,' wrote Evelyn. Tuesday saw the disappearance of the Royal Exchange and Guildhall. (Mercifuly, the city documents, stored in the basement of Guildhall, were preserved.) St. Paul's turn came in the evening.

From the surrounding bookshops in Paternoster Row thousands of books had. been carried down to St. Faith's-under-Paul's, beneath the cathedral's floor. Unfortunately, the hope that the churchyard would act as a fire-break proved unfounded; the merchants didn't help matters by using it as a depository for their goods. Nor did the wooden scaffolding which was covering the cathedral, which was in the process of being restored. It was this that caught alight first. When the lead of the roof reached melting point, it poured to the ground in a cascading torrent, the sheer weight of the metal causing the floor to collapse. The books stored in St. Faith's then added to the blaze. Very soon the great church, for centuries at the heart of the City's existence, both as a place of worship and a centre of commerce, was reduced to a shell of smouldering rubble. Evelyn wrote: 'The stones of Paules flew like granados, the melting lead running downe the streetes in a streame, and the very pavements flowing with fiery rednesse . . . the Eastern Wind still more impetuously driving the flames forward'.

The same night the wind fell. In the east, fears that it would now change direction occasioned anxiety. Samuel Pepys was living in Seething Lane, near the Navy Office in Crutched Friars, where he worked. At 2 a.m. on the Wednesday morning Mrs. Pepys woke here husband to tell him of nearby shouts of fire. Samuel rose, gathered together his large fortune in gold, and took it by boat to the safety of the village of Woolwich. He needn't have troubled himself. Admiral Sir William Penn, a close friend of Pepys, ordered the large-scale blowing-up of houses by dockyard workers (for which a magazine of powder lying in the White Tower was used). As a result, the advance of the fire was halted at the porch of All Hallows, where the admiral's son, the future Quaker, had been baptised. When the bombs showered down in the Second World War, this historic church enjoyed no such escape. Nor did St. Olave's, Hart Street, another survivor of the Great Fire, where the Pepyses worshipped and were laid to rest. In the west the flames were finally checked when they had almost reached Temple Bar.

By Friday the citizens were in a position to take stock of the size of the calamity; 396 acres of houses had been destroyed, comprising 400 streets, 13,200 dwellings, 89 churches and four of the city gates. The value of the property lost was almost incalculable. The effect of the disaster was substantially to erase the medieval city of London. The Earl of Clarendon wrote:

> Above two parts of three of that great city were burned to ashes, and those the most rich and wealthy parts of the city, where the greatest warehouses and the best shops stood. The Royal Exchange, with all the streets about it, Lombard-Street, Cheapside, Paternoster-Row, St. Paul's church, and almost all the other churches in the city, with the Old Bailey, Ludgate, all Paul's churchyard even to the Thames, and the greatest part of Fleet-Street, all which were places the best inhabited, were all burned down without one house remaining.

The fire had almost certainly started by chance, but the truth wasn't psychologically satisfying. Scapegoats had to be looked for. Foreigners and Catholics were the obvious outlets for a people's frenzied bewilderment. Among those hanged was a Frenchman who, it was later discovered, had arrived in England only after the fire had begun its work of devastation. An inscription on the Monument attributing the fire to a Catholic conspiracy would cause Alexander Pope to comment:

> London's column pointing
>   to the skies,
> Like a tall bully lifts
>   its head and lies.

In 1830 the fabrication was finally removed on the order of the Common Council.

The Monument has a Latin inscription: 'London rises again, whether with greater speed or greater magnificence is doubtful; three short years complete that which was considered the work of an

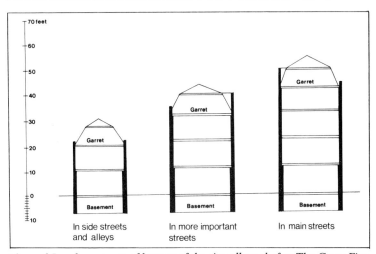

Planned London – types of houses of the size allowed after The Great Fire

age.' This isn't true; for example, St. Paul's was not finished till 1710. Yet a remarkable amount was achieved in a short time. After three years most people had roofs over their heads. The merchants saw to it that the Royal Exchange was quick to reappear. The creation of King and Queen Streets gave Guildhall direct access to the river. The speed of recovery was partly due to an influx of craftsmen and labourers. These new arrivals were not liked by the older residents. In spite of its cosmopolitan character, London had never warmed to 'foreigns'. All the same, to cope with the disaster, guild privileges were temporarily relaxed.

The Rebuilding Act of February 1667 is a landmark in the history of town-planning. Sizes of house were prescribed for types of street: two-storey houses were allowed in side streets, three-storey houses in wider but not principal streets, four-storey houses in high streets. The Act laid down the vital principle of the building line, which put an end to the jutting-out frontages and spouting gutters of medieval London. It also created a special Fire Court, which deliberated at Clifford's Inn in Fleet Street. This had the power to deal summarily with all the claims and counter-claims from the fire; the ordinary processes of law wouldn't suffice.

Many years later John Woodward, MD, Gresham Lecturer in Physic, wrote a letter congratulating Sir Christopher Wren on his role in the rebuilding. Though a disaster for the inhabitants, the fire 'had prov'd infinitely beneficial to their Posterity; conducing vastly to the Improvment and Increase, as well of the Riches and

Opulency, as of the Splendour of this City. Then which I and every Body must observe with great Satisfaction, by means of the Inlargements of the streets; of the great Plenty of good Water, convey'd to all Parts; of the common Sewers, and other like Contrivances; such Provision is made for a free access and Passage of the Air, for Sweetness, for Cleanness, and for Salubrity, that it is not only the finest, but the most healthy City in the world.'

St. Paul's Cathedral

The first authenticated St. Paul's was founded in the early 7th century by Bishop Mellitus and endowed by Ethelbert, king of Kent. This church was burned down in 1087. Its successor, Old St. Paul's, even bigger than the present cathedral, took two centuries to complete. Its spire surmounted the central tower and reached to a height of 493 feet. This was burned down in 1561.

For centuries St. Paul's was a centre of trade as well as a place of worship. Merchants did their business in the nave. (Shakespeare makes Falstaff say of Bardolph, 'I bought him in St. Paul's'.) When the reformers gained control, they removed the relics and the rood screen, but not the merchants, who continued to meet in the nave, or Paul's Walk, even after the opening of Gresham's Bourse in 1568.

For a long period the church was neglected. Then restoration began under Charles I, Inigo Jones designing a classical portico for the west front. In 1666 the cathedral was virtually burned down in the Great Fire. The present cathedral, designed by Sir Christopher Wren, was not completed until 1710. During the Second World War it miraculously escaped serious damage.

St. Paul's is about half the size of St. Peter's in Rome, which it resembles. It is built of Portland Stone in the shape of a Latin Cross (Wren would have preferred a Greek Cross, i.e. a cross with four equal arms, but this didn't please the High Church party).

On the west side, looking down Ludgate Hill, is the imposing double portico. Note the pediment on which is a bas-relief by Francis Bird representing the conversion of St. Paul. On the apex stands a statue of St. Paul, with St. Peter on his right and St. James on the left. In the north tower there is a peal of twelve bells, presented by City companies. In the south, or clock-tower, is Great Paul, the largest bell in the Commonwealth. It is rung for five minutes daily at one o'clock.

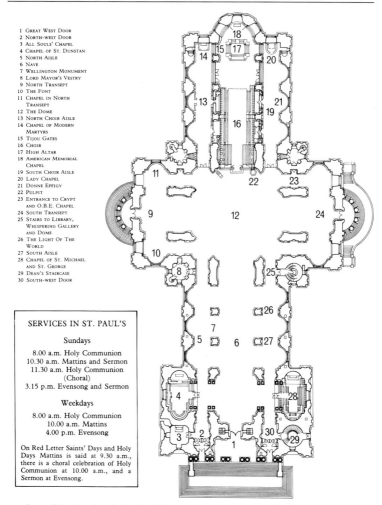

1 GREAT WEST DOOR
2 NORTH-WEST DOOR
3 ALL SOULS' CHAPEL
4 CHAPEL OF ST. DUNSTAN
5 NORTH AISLE
6 NAVE
7 WELLINGTON MONUMENT
8 LORD MAYOR'S VESTRY
9 NORTH TRANSEPT
10 THE FONT
11 CHAPEL IN NORTH
   TRANSEPT
12 THE DOME
13 NORTH CHOIR AISLE
14 CHAPEL OF MODERN
   MARTYRS
15 TIJOU GATES
16 CHOIR
17 HIGH ALTAR
18 AMERICAN MEMORIAL
   CHAPEL
19 SOUTH CHOIR AISLE
20 LADY CHAPEL
21 DONNE EFFIGY
22 PULPIT
23 ENTRANCE TO CRYPT
   AND O.B.E. CHAPEL
24 SOUTH TRANSEPT
25 STAIRS TO LIBRARY,
   WHISPERING GALLERY
   AND DOME
26 THE LIGHT OF THE
   WORLD
27 SOUTH AISLE
28 CHAPEL OF ST. MICHAEL
   AND ST. GEORGE
29 DEAN'S STAIRCASE
30 SOUTH-WEST DOOR

SERVICES IN ST. PAUL'S

Sundays

8.00 a.m. Holy Communion
10.30 a.m. Mattins and Sermon
11.30 a.m. Holy Communion
(Choral)
3.15 p.m. Evensong and Sermon

Weekdays

8.00 a.m. Holy Communion
10.00 a.m. Mattins
4.00 p.m. Evensong

On Red Letter Saints' Days and Holy
Days Mattins is said at 9.30 a.m.,
there is a choral celebration of Holy
Communion at 10.00 a.m., and a
Sermon at Evensong.

A plan of St. Paul's Cathedral (The Registrar, St. Paul's Cathedral)

Go to the south porch (Cannon Street side). Note the five statues of apostles and, in the pediment, a phoenix with the motto 'Resurgam' ('I shall rise again'). When Wren was wanting to indicate the centre of the dome space, he was brought a fragment of a tombstone from a pile of charred remains. It carried this single word.

You can see the outer dome of timber covered with lead. There are two more. The inner dome of brick is low enough for Thornhill's murals to be appreciated. Between them is a conical dome, also of brick, supporting the lantern and the ball and cross.

The Interior Walk up the centre of the nave to the space beneath the dome. The ceiling of the inner dome is decorated with eight paintings by Sir James Thornhill, showing scenes from the life of St. Paul. The spandrels between the arches are covered by eight large mosaics. At a lower level, mosaics also adorn the quarter-domes. Above the arches is the **Whispering Gallery**. In the niches above this gallery are statues of the Fathers of the Church.

Don't overlook the statue of Dr Johnson. On the right is the new pulpit designed by Lord Mottistone. On the right side of the south choir aisle is the figure of Dr John Donne (1573–1631), poet and Dean of St. Paul's. This survived the destruction of Old St. Paul's, and it still shows traces of fire. The choir stalls and the organ case are carved by Grinling Gibbons. The fine iron gates by Jean Tijou lead to the apse, occupied by the **Jesus Chapel**, a memorial to Americans who lost their lives in the Second World War.

The **Crypt** extends beneath the entire church. The east end forms what used to be called the chapel of St. Faith. When Old St. Paul's was built, the church of St. Faith was demolished to make room for the choir, and the parishioners were given the chapel as their parish church. Nelson's body is preserved in spirit in the great tomb under the centre of the dome. The 16th-century marble sarcophagus was originally intended for Wolsey, and later Henry VIII. The coffin is made from the mainmast of the French flagship at the battle of Aboukir Bay. At the west end, the tomb of Wellington is a great block of porphyry resting on a granite base. The Iron Duke's funeral car is cast from cannon captured by him. Before leaving the crypt find Wren's tombstone in Painters' Corner.

The **Library and Galleries** are reached from the south aisle. The steps lead to the **South Triforium Gallery**. The library possesses a promise signed by Charles II of £1,000 a year towards the rebuilding fund. The **Trophy Room**, reached from the West Gallery, contains models and drawings by Wren, including the **Great Model**.

Continue your ascent to the Whispering Gallery, good vantage point for a study of Thornhill's paintings. The next flight of steps leads to the **Stone Gallery**, the exterior gallery round the base of the dome. The view is even better from the **Golden Gallery** at the base of the lantern.

The Vicinity of the Cathedral A vast area to the north of St. Paul's was devastated on 29 December 1940. Today shops and office blocks have replaced the pre-war streets. The old names –

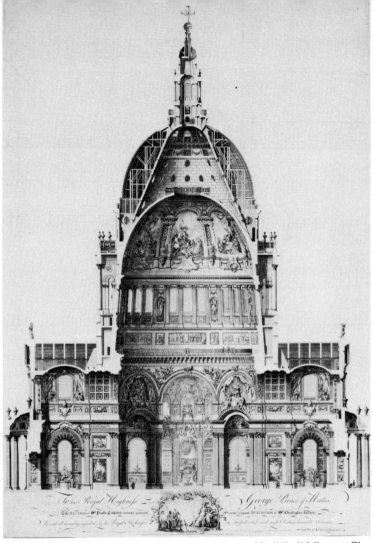

A section of St. Paul's showing Wren's three domes (Guildhall Library, City of London)

transmitters of ancient associations – survive: Paternoster Row, Amen Court, Ave Maria Lane and Creed Lane. The modern Paternoster Square is a shopping precinct. Wren's Chapter House survived the Blitz. To the south, in Dean's Court, is the Deanery, also built by Wren.

The churchyard, where the Folkmoot used to assemble, is now a public garden. In the north-east corner is the site of Paul's Cross. Nearby there is a memorial cross.

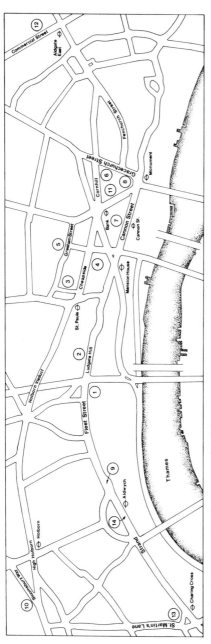

Churches by Wren, Hawksmoor and Gibbs

Wren
1. St. Bride's, Fleet Street
2. St. Martin Ludgate, Ludgate Hill
3. St. Vedast, Foster Lane
4. St. Mary-le-Bow, Cheapside
5. St. Lawrence Jewry, Gresham Street
6. St. Peter, Cornhill
7. St. Stephen Walbrook
8. St. Clement, Eastcheap
9. St. Clement Danes, The Strand

Hawksmoor
10. St. George's Bloomsbury
11. St. Mary Woolnoth, Lombard Street
12. Christ Church, Spitalfields

Gibbs
13. St. Martin's-in-the-Fields, Trafalgar Square
14. St. Mary-le-Strand

Churches of Wren, Hawskmoor and Gibbs*

A Wren sample:
ST. BRIDE'S, FLEET STREET
The tallest city spire – 226 feet. The undercroft, showing the foundations of seven previous churches on the site, is open to the public.

ST. MARTIN LUDGATE, LUDGATE HILL

ST. VEDAST, FOSTER LANE
(the Goldsmiths' church)

ST. MARY-LE-BOW, CHEAPSIDE
Probably only the tower and steeple are by Wren. There is a Norman crypt.

ST. LAWRENCE JEWRY, GRESHAM STREET

ST. PETER, CORNHILL

ST. STEPHEN WALBROOK

ST. CLEMENT EASTCHEAP
Serves the City's smallest parish. ('Oranges and lemons says the bells of St. Clements' – St. Clement Eastcheap or St. Clement Danes?)

ST. CLEMENT DANES, THE STRAND
(Spire by Gibbs)

ST. JAMES'S, PICCADILLY

Six by Wren's pupil, Nicholas Hawksmoor:
ST. GEORGE'S, BLOOMSBURY

ST. MARY WOOLNOTH, LOMBARD STREET

CHRIST CHURCH, SPITALFIELDS

ST. GEORGE-IN-THE-EAST, CANNON STREET ROAD

ST. ANNE, LIMEHOUSE

ST. ALFEGE, GREENWICH

ST. MARTIN-IN-THE-FIELDS, TRAFALGAR SQUARE and
ST. MARY-LE-STRAND were built in the same period by James Gibbs.

* See Mervyn Blatch, *A Guide to London's Churches* (Constable, 1978).

Bunhill Fields, City Road

Bunhill fields – the name is derived from Bonehill – is the Noncomformist burial ground, aptly described by Robert Southey as the 'Campo Santo' of Dissenters. Here you will find the graves of John Bunyan, Daniel Defoe and William Blake. There is a separate Quaker burial ground, to which the plain wooden coffin of George Fox, the founder of Quakerism, was brought in 1691. In the City Road, which runs past Bunhill Fields on the east, is the chapel where John Wesley, the founder of Methodism, used to preach. His remarkable mother, Suzannah, who bore him, Charles and seventeen others, is buried in Bunhill Fields. To the west, in Bunhill Row, the blind John Milton lived from 1662 until his death in 1672, finishing *Paradise Lost* and writing *Paradise Regained.*

Downing Street

In 1660, the year of the Stuart Restoration, Samuel Pepys described Sir George Downing as so stingy a fellow that he cared not to see him. At that time Pepys worked as his clerk at the Exchequer. Downing was certainly an opportunist. Having been a Parliamentarian of distinction, he was ever so quick to make his peace with Charles II, securing a knighthood in the process. The famous street was developed by Downing in Whitehall on land which he purchased in 1681. In 1735 No. 10 became the official residence of the First Lord of the Treasury (the PM), who at that time was Sir Robert Walpole. No. 11 is the official residence of the Chancellor of the Exchequer. No. 12 is the Goverment Whip's Office, from where the steps descend to St. James's Park.

The Royal Hospital, Chelsea

Wren's Royal Hospital, which comprises buildings forming three quadrangles, was founded by Charles II in 1682 for the benefit of army veterans, who may be seen in their scarlet coats in the summer or their dark blue greatcoats in winter. The hospital grounds, leading down to the river, are adjoined to the east by Ranelagh Gardens. In their 18th-century heyday these were famous pleasure gardens with a great rotunda, complementing the rather less fashionable Vauxhall pleasure gardens on the Surrey side.

The Royal Naval College Park and Observatory, Greenwich

The Royal Naval College, consisting of four separate blocks, occupies the site of a royal palace – the **Palace of Placentia** – built in the 15th century. It was similar to Hampton Court and nearly as big. Here Henry VIII and his daughters, Mary and Elizabeth, were born, and Edward VI died. Charles II started to rebuild the palace, but did not get far. At the request of Queen Mary, the wife of William of Orange (1688–1702), the palace was converted into a hospital for disabled seamen. The building was carried out by Christopher Wren. The hospital was closed in 1869 and the buildings subsequently taken over by the Admiralty for the education of naval officers. Under one of the twin domes (south west block) is the **Painted Hall**, built by Wren with florid ceiling paintings by Sir James Thornhill of St. Paul's fame. The other

Chelsea Hospital (Guildhall Library, City of London)

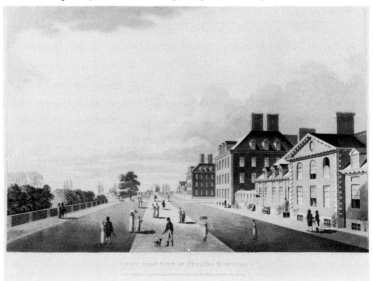

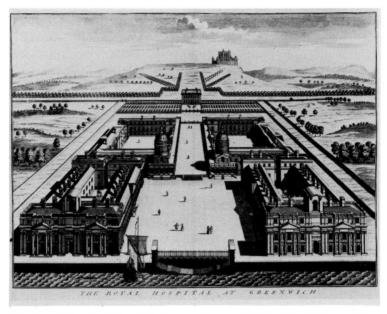

The Royal Hospital (Naval College) at Greenwich (Guildhall Library, City of London)

(south-east block) belongs to the **Chapel**, which is also open to the public.

South of the National Maritime Museum is Greenwich Park, a royal domain of 185 acres. The oldest of the London parks, it was enclosed in the 15th century and laid out by Le Nôtre in the reign of Charles II. On a hill in the centre is the **Greenwich Observatory** founded in 1675 with the aim of providing seamen with reliable data for determining their positions at sea. The zero meridian of longitude (marked on the path north of the gates) passes through Greenwich, and 'Greenwich time' is still the official mean time for Great Britain. Daily at 1.00 p.m. a time-ball falls on a mast on the roof of **Flamsteed House** built by Wren to house John Flamsteed (1646–1719), the first astronomer royal. Constructed in 1833, it was the world's first visual time-signal, designed to enable masters of ships in the London docks and chronometer-makers in Clerkenwell to check their chronometers without having to take them to the observatory.

Kensington Palace and Gardens

William of Orange disliked crowds and sought the peace of the countryside. As an asthmatic, he found the Whitehall air unhealthy. Therefore, he bought Nottingham House, situated on rising ground near the village of Kensington. Wren (who else?) was brought in to give it the look of a palace. William and Mary, Anne (1702–14) and George II (1727–60) all died there. Until the death of George II it was a residence of the reigning sovereign. Queen Victoria was born in the Palace (1819) and lived there until her accession.

Kensington Gardens, once the private gardens of the palace, lie to the west of Hyde Park, from which they were taken. Queen Caroline, wife of George II, created the Serpentine, which divides the two parks. The entire area of both these 'lungs of London',

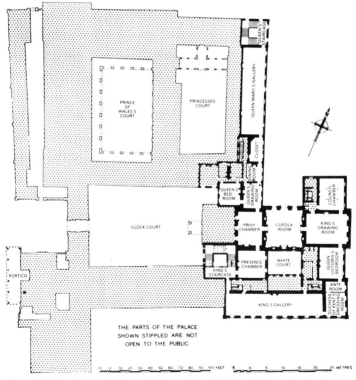

A plan of Kensington Palace (Controller of Her Majesty's Stationery Office)

William III's country retreat – a 19th century view of Kensington Palace
(Guildhall Library, City of London)

which was originally the property of the Abbot of Westminster, had passed to the Crown at the time of the Dissolution of the Monasteries.

Fenton House, Hampstead

Built on the west side of Hampstead Heath in 1693, its treasures include a collection of 18th-century porcelain, some early keyboard instruments, including a harpsichord played by Handel, and a painting of Hampstead Heath by Constable.

Fenton House – stately living in Hampstead (Tom Picton)

Marlborough House, off the Mall

This red-bricked mansion was built by Sir Christopher Wren (1709–11) for the Duke of Marlborough, the victor at Blenheim (1704), and his wife, Sarah Churchill. Sarah wanted an impressive gate. Sir Robert Walpole, the Prime Minister, frustrated her scheme by buying some houses that were in the way. He didn't have an impressive gate at No. 10 – why should she? She never forgave him. Look for the entrance at the west end of Pall Mall.

135

Marlborough House – palatial prize for Queen Anne's victorious duke (Guildhall Library, City of London)

Markets

Covent Garden was developed by the fourth Earl of Bedford in 1632. The fifth Earl built sheds against his garden wall and leased them out to the sellers of fruit and vegetables. In 1671 a charter was obtained from Charles II. The market was to outgrow every other London market except Smithfield. The main market-buildings were erected in the 1830s. The fruit and vegetable sellers winged their way to Nine Elms south of the river in 1974, and the area was taken over by shops, eating places and street performers, ranging from clowns to cellists. The piazza's link with entertainment isn't new – Pepys witnessed a Punch and Judy show in front of St. Paul's portico. The London Transport Museum was opened in 1980 in the former flower market in the south-east of the square.

Spitalfields, Brushfield Street, E1 Also a fruit and vegetable market, and likewise established by a charter of Charles II.

9 London since the 18th century

In the 1760s the city gates, long since obstacles to the free flow of traffic, and a recognized anachronism, were finally pulled down. The gate at Temple Bar remained till 1878, when it was removed to Waltham Cross in Hertfordshire.

No overall plan directed the burgeoning growth of London. However, the West End of the 17th and 18th centuries, unlike the East End, wasn't shaped in an entirely haphazard and piecemeal way. The land to the west of the city, which had mainly belonged to Westminster Abbey, had passed chiefly into the hands of a small number of aristocrats, who planned the laying out of the squares and the streets which radiated from them. Land was often let in plots to builders on long leases and at a low ground rent on condition that houses of a prescribed kind should be erected. A major scheme such as Bedford Square and its surrounding network of streets wouldn't have been possible in the east, where there were no major landowners like the Russells.

An earlier member of the Russell family had built up Covent Garden before the Civil War. After the Restoration, Bloomsbury Square had been created by the Earl of St. Albans, who considered that 'The beauty of this great town and the convenience of the Court are defective in houses fit for the dwellings of noblemen.'

The requirements of less exalted customers were of concern to a speculative builder such as Dr Nicholas Barbon, who had a large hand in the development of the Bedford estate. The system of building leases, which enabled Barbon to grow rich, gave rise from the early days of Covent Garden and Lincoln's Inn Fields to the London terrace house, designed, as is the tower block, to make maximum use of the available space.

The focal points of London's western growth were the squares. To Dr Johnson, who spent much of his time in and around Fleet Street, they probably seemed remote; men moved to Grosvenor Square, or to Berkeley Square, to 'get away from it all'. He never knew Fitzroy Square (the south and east sides were built by Robert

George Jones's 1815 Map (simplified) showing main estates and the interests of families in various areas

The Royal Adelphi Terrace fronting the Thames (Guildhall Library, City of London)

and James Adam in the 1790s, the other sides not being completed until the 1820s, or Russell Square (named after the Russells, Earls and Dukes of Bedford), Gordon Square and Tavistock Square, which didn't appear until the 19th century. More remote, yet to be eventually absorbed into what William Cobbett would call 'the Infernal Wen', were growing villages like Hampstead, famous for its spring, Highgate, Wandsworth and Fulham. Lord Burlington's new villa at Chiswick and Horace Walpole's Strawberry Hill at Twickenham were still in the depths of the countryside.

The fashionable West End mirrored the taste of its creators. Classical elegance was the order of the day. The aesthetic watchwords were uniformity and simplicity. The chief influence was Inigo Jones, though his strict adherence to the classical rules hadn't won general favour. There's nothing so rigid about the architecture of Christopher Wren or of Robert and James Adam, whose most extensive work was the Adelphi, south of the Strand. This was a magnificent riverside terrace, called the Royal Adelphi Terrace, erected on an arched embankment, winged by two more terraces running back from the river. It was modelled on the palace of Diocletian overlooking the Adriatic which Robert had seen in 1757. David Garrick purchased No. 5, the centre house on the Royal

Carlton House with its screening colonnade of paired Ionic columns (Guildhall Library, City of London)

Adelphi Terrace. Most of the houses, however, were slow to sell. In 1936 the Adelphi was demolished to make way for an office block. The names of Adam, John Adam and Robert Streets recall the brothers' almost vanished creation. Though the Adams' influence was widespread, not all architects followed so individual an approach. Two new buildings of the period, George Dance's Mansion House in the city, and Sir William Chambers's Somerset House in the Strand, were both strictly formal in design.

Much Georgian architecture has been spoiled or destroyed. The Victorians disliked its plainness and uniformity. Property developers in the 20th century – like their predecessors – have often shown scant regard for the past. Some surviving Georgian oases are Church Row in Hampstead, Bedford Square by the British Museum, Goodwin's Court near Trafalgar Square, and Lord North Street, near Westminster Abbey.

In the early 1780s Prince George, the future Prince Regent, left St. James's Palace and moved to nearby Carlton House, on the north-east side of St. James's Park. The site couldn't be bettered, though the house itself was rather dull. The Prince enlisted the help of the architect Henry Holland, and soon the plain brick building was transformed into an elegantly designed palace, screened from the crowds passing down Pall Mall by a colonnade of paired Ionic columns with two impressive gateways. 'You cannot call it magnificent; it is the taste and the propriety that strike . . .' wrote the elderly Horace Walpole.

Taste and propriety are the hallmarks of Regency London, which may be said to last from George's move to Carlton House until the Victorian era. The Regent's world was one of a self-conscious fashionableness typified by the Regency dandy, whose pre-occupation with style and appearance could be carried to the absurd lengths of the legendary Beau Brummell.

The Regent's world didn't impinge on the East End. Since the East End was the principal point of arrival in the capital, it was based in part on the hard work of immigrant labour. The value of London's exports and imports in 1800 was estimated at the huge figure of £70 million. Trade had trebled in the previous century. But for widespread smuggling, the returns would have been even greater. To beat the smugglers, who operated on the many wharves, a major dock-building programme was begun. Surrounded by high walls and protected by armed guards, these docks gave the smuggler no chance. Now they are largely relics being redeveloped, or awaiting redevelopment. The West India Dock in the Isle of Dogs was the first to be constructed (in 1802), soon to be followed by the

The Opening of the St. Katharine Dock in 1825. It is now a yacht harbour and marine museum (Guildhall Library, City of London)

141

London Dock at Wapping, the East India at Blackwall, and (on the south side) the Surrey. In 1825 over a thousand dilapidated houses immediately east of the Tower, together with the medieval buildings of St. Katharine's Hospital, were demolished to make way for St. Katharine's Dock, designed by the great road-builder Thomas Telford.

The East End was quickly transformed. The riverside hamlets became indistinguishable parts of an unbroken dormitory for dock workers. Commercial Road and the East India Dock Road were constructed for the dock traffic, with the result that the old east-west routes of Cable Street, the Ratcliff Highway and Poplar High Street became shadows of their former selves. Later came the Regent's Canal, and then the railways, while the population would be swollen by two major influxes – the hungry Irish in the 1840s and eventually fugitive Jews from Russia.

The Scotsman, John Rennie, who helped to design the West India Dock, was responsible for three new bridges: Southwark, Waterloo and Vauxhall. Of these Waterloo, with its nine semi-elliptical arches and pairs of Doric columns, was the finest. It was demolished in 1927. Rennie also designed a new London Bridge, which his sons completed in 1831. This London Bridge, the second to be made of stone, was demolished and sold to the Americans in 1969. (It is now in Arizona.) Of John Rennie's work only the graceful bridge across the Serpentine has been allowed to survive.

Rennie's more remembered contemporary, John Nash, might have lived his days in comparative obscurity but for marrying a young (and pregnant) mistress of the Prince. His first royal commission was to design a new conservatory in the garden of the Brighton Pavilion. Eight years later, in 1806, Nash became an architect in the department of Woods and Forests. In 1811, the year in which the Prince became Regent, the expiration of Crown leases of the farmlands covering Marylebone Park, a large area to the north of the New Road, gave the ambitious, though elderly, Nash his golden opportunity. He was essentially not an architect, but a town-planner with a visionary eye for the grand design. In this respect he may be compared to Wren, with his great scheme for London after the Fire. When the architects of the department of Woods and Forests were asked to submit their own ideas for the future development of Marylebone Park, it was Nash's report which embodied the radical and imaginative conception. Unlike Wren's, Nash's scheme was accepted. The Regent enthused over it, though the Treasury dragged its feet. Nash's development started in the north with Regent's Park and his imposing surrounding terraces

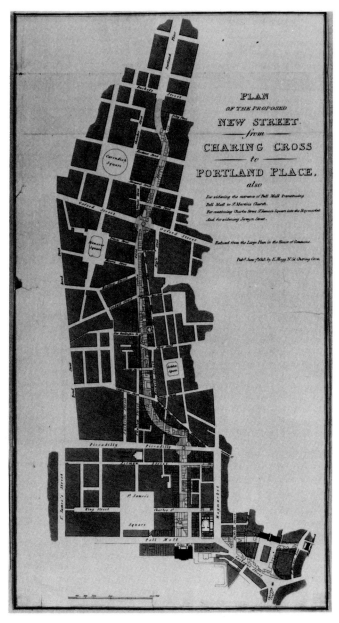

Plan of Regent Street 1813 (Guildhall Library, City of London)

which may be seen today. A summer villa intended for the Regent never transpired. Cumberland Terrace was given a special grandeur, because it was going to be opposite this royal retreat from the hubbub of Pall Mall. On the park's eastern side was the Park Village, supplied by Nash's Regent's Canal, which ran from the Grand Junction at Paddington to Limehouse in the East End, thus linking Thamesside with the Midlands and the North.

Connecting Carlton House with Regent's Park, Regent Street originally consisted of buildings designed by Nash. Property rights dictated the layout of the scheme. This was because it was necessary to avoid buildings which could not be purchased. A straight line wasn't possible as a result. Piccadilly Circus and the Quadrant, a quarter circle with colonnades on either side, were designed to lead Regent Street to its realignment near the Carlton House end. At the junction with Oxford Street Nash placed a second circus. His All Souls church with its circular portico took away the ungraceful sharpness from the bend into Portland Place.

The Adams' Portland Place, one of the widest streets in London, lies to the south of Regent's Park. Its Adam houses have been gradually disappearing. Nash's Regent Street has also fared badly, for though the overall scheme survives, its original architecture does not. The Victorians removed the colonnades from the Quadrant because they (supposedly) encouraged prostitution as well as darkening the shops. By 1927 all of Nash's buildings in Regent Street had been destroyed.

To enhance the beauty of the approach from Westminster to Charing Cross, Nash suggested that 'a square or crescent, open to and looking down Parliament Street, might be built round the Equestrian statue at Charing Cross'. So to him we owe the broad conception of Trafalgar Square. Not until 1829 was a start made on it. From then on the execution was both protracted and piecemeal. By 1841 the area had been laid out. The Nelson Column, begun in 1840, took three years to erect. Edwin Landseer's lions did not arrive until 1867.

Nash landscaped St. James's Park, turning the canal into a lake. Carlton House, on which so much money had been spent, was discarded in favour of a scheme to convert Buckingham House, built in 1703 and later bought by George III, into a magnificent palace. Nash's even more magnificent entrance gate was much later removed to the end of Oxford Street, where we know it as Marble Arch. To raise funds Carlton House was demolished. It was replaced by the Terrace, designed by Nash.

*   *   *   *   *   *

Nash's London – Regent Street Quadrant 1852 (Guildhall Library, City of London)

The First Buck House (Guildhall Library, City of London)

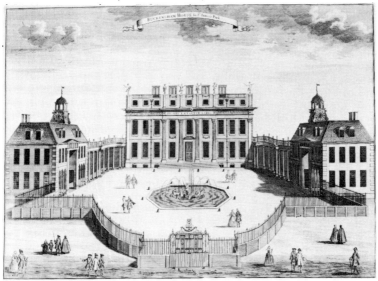

> But, how is this Wen to be dispersed I know not whether it be to
> be done by knife or by caustic; but, dispersed it must be!
>
> William Cobbett, *Rural Rides*

When Victoria ascended the throne in 1837, London had become
Cobbett's 'Infernal Wen'. Parts were less infernal than a hundred
years before, when Johnson and Garrick had arrived. In many ways
the 18th century had been an age of improvement, a break with the
lingering medieval past. In 1733 the smelly Fleet was covered.
Rounded cobbles gradually disappeared and gutters were built
either side of the road. Raised pavements for pedestrians,
previously protected by a line of posts at best, became usual for the
first time. The large shop signs were taken down, and houses began
to be numbered. Soon there was to be an improvement in street
lighting. In 1802 gas lighting was demonstrated in Soho, and before
long it was installed in Pall Mall. In 1814 it came to Piccadilly.

London continued to spread, but sometimes tastefully. The
greatest entrepreneurial builder of the early 19th century was
Thomas Cubitt, 'the emperor of the building trade', who extended
Bloomsbury to the New (line of Euston) road by way of his Gordon
and Tavistock Squares. Cubitt's other contribution was Belgravia, a
project which stemmed from the rebuilding of Buckingham House.
The new development lay on the marshy ground to the east of
Sloane Street, the route which from the 1780s linked Knightsbridge
with Chelsea. Belgrave and Eaton Squares became as fashionable
as Mayfair, the 18th century area of development which lay to the
north, bordered by Park Lane, Oxford Street, Regent Street and
Piccadilly. Belgravia and much of Mayfair formed part of the
Grosvenor estate.

In complete contrast was the slum area of St. Giles Rookery,
Dickens's 'Tom-All-Alone's', partly erased by the construction of
New Oxford Street. Victoria Street (begun in 1852) connected
Parliament Square with the vicinity of Buckingham Palace. Such
developments befitted Victorian London's status as the capital of
the hugely expanding empire. So did the Victoria Embankment
from Westminster to Blackfriars. Underneath ran two emblems of
Victorian improvement: a railway (the District) and three sewers.
The problem of sanitation had for years been aggravated by the
appearance in the capital of the flushing lavatory. A huge amount of
waste was now carried to the Thames. After 1848, when the use of
cesspits was forbidden, the Thames took it all. The water supply,
most of which was drawn from the river, was even more polluted
than before. In the hot June of 1858 people crossing Westminster

Buckingham Palace (Guildhall Library, City of London)

The Great Wen – Tallis's Illustrated Plan of London and its environs 1851 (Guildhall Library, City of London)

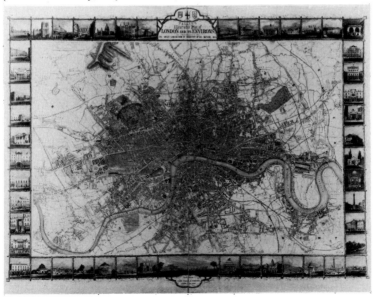

Still beyond The Wen – Highgate from Holloway 1859 (Guildhall Library, City of London)

The Last of the Fleet (Guildhall Library, City of London)

Gaslit London (Guildhall Library, City of London)

Bridge had to hold their noses. Confronted by 'the Great Stink', the members of Parliament found their working environment impossibly uncongenial. It was this situation rather than the outbreaks of cholera which finally induced Parliament to take belated action. From choice most members would have followed *The Times* in preferring to take their 'chance of cholera and the rest than be bullied into health'. (A year later (1859) Dr John Snow confirmed his theory that cholera was carried by unclean water when he showed that all the cholera victims in an area of Soho had taken water from the same pump.)

Joseph Bazalgette, Chief Engineer of the Metropolitan Board of Works, set up in 1855, was employed to deal with the crisis. Bazalgette suggested that sewers should be built alongside the river (three on the north and two on the south) to meet the others before they discharged. The sewage would not be released until it reached the estuary. A stretch of the sewers on the north side was incorporated beneath a new road and embankment along the waterfront. Between 1864 and 1870 Bazalgette constructed the mile-and-a-half Victoria Embankment from Westminster Bridge (incidentally, not Wordsworth's since this one was rebuilt between 1854 and 1862) to Blackfriars Bridge (rebuilt between 1865 and 1869). From here the road, becoming Queen Victoria Street, continued through the city to the Mansion House. A continuous route now linked the two ancient seats of authority. Northumberland Avenue, connecting the embankment with Trafalgar Square, entailed the demolition of Northumberland House (1605), the last of the great private houses on the south side of the Strand, where rich and powerful Tudor laymen, like the Cecils, Raleigh and the Earl of Essex, had superseded the bishops. Some names in the area, such as Arundel Street and Essex Street, recall departed splendours. The 1880s saw the creation of Shaftesbury Avenue (named after the Victorian philanthropist) and the Charing Cross Road. More of St. Giles Rookery and other slums disappeared in the process.

The London which we know took shape in the reigns of Victoria and Edward VII. Victorians and Edwardians built the National Gallery (1838), the new Palace of Westminster (1839–60), the South Kensington museums (from 1851), the Government offices in Whitehall (from 1861), the Albert Embankment (1869), the Albert Hall (1871), the Chelsea Embankment (1872), Albert Bridge (1873), Wandsworth Bridge (1873), Tower Bridge (1894), Westminster Cathedral (1903) and Harrods (1905).

Eclectic Victorian taste, rejecting the uniformity of the Georgian

Jacobean Northumberland House on the south side of the Strand will not survive the Victorian Age of Improvement (Guildhall Library, City of London)

period, added a mixture of styles to London's architecture. The revival of interest in medieval Gothic produced some remarkable buildings: notably, Sir Charles Barry's Palace of Westminster, built after fire had destroyed the old one in 1834, Sir Gilbert Scott's St. Pancras Station, and the Law Courts in the Strand. Gothic, predominant for a while, took its place alongside many other styles. Nothing could be less like St. Pancras than the Royal Albert Hall. This future shrine of the promenaders was built, as were the South Kensington Museums, on thirty acres of land purchased by the Government out of the profit from the Great Exhibition (1851) held in Joseph Paxton's huge Crystal Palace in Hyde Park, where the concrete foundations remain under the grass. The great glass structure was removed to Sydenham, where it was destroyed by fire in 1936. A turret clock from the exhibition is on King's Cross Station. In Kensington Gardens stands the Albert Memorial, a reminder not only of the Prince Consort, who inspired the exhibition, but of Sir Gilbert Scott, the memorial's designer, and the neo-Gothic revival.

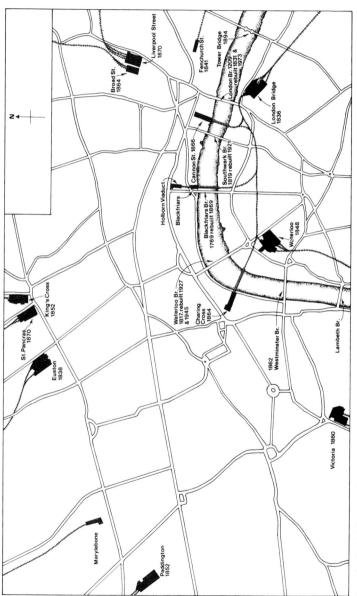

London's Bridges and Main Line Stations (Guildhall Library, City of London)

The poor are displaced, but they are not removed. They are shovelled out of one side of the parish, only to render more overcrowded the stifling apartments in another part . . .
The Times 1861 on the effect of the railways on the London poor

The railways were the most significant Victorian contribution to the development of the capital. This shining symbol of progress conferred undoubted benefits, but was also, as *The Times* extract reminds us, an agent of destruction and squalor.

London's first railway was the Southwark and Greenwich (1836), and soon London Bridge station was being used by other lines. In 1841 the City Corporation allowed the London and Blackwall to run into Fenchurch Street, creating a quick route from the East and West India Docks to the City. It was to provide a link with the docks (from the London (Euston) and Birmingham Railway) that the North London Line was conceived later on. In fact, the importance of this line, built in an arc from Broad Street at the eastern end of the city, via Hampstead and Finchley, to Richmond, lies in the creation of commuterdom.

By 1870 four railway bridges and all the great London stations were in existence: Euston (1838), Waterloo (1848), King's Cross and Paddington (1852), Victoria (1860), Charing Cross and Broad Street (1864), Cannon Street (1866) and the two neo-Gothic constructions, St. Pancras (1870) and Liverpool Street (1870), the latter on the medieval site of the Bethlehem Hospital for the insane.

The railways helped to create the dormitory suburbs, especially after the introduction of cheap fares for workmen. Willesden provides a case study. Owing to the North London Railway, its population rose from 16,000 in 1871 to almost 115,000 in 1901. Commuterdom, as we know it, had been born. The City's population declined. Office blocks took the place of houses. At night streets where businessmen had lived above their work were deserted. As for the Infernal Wen, it became, in the description of Lord Rosebery, speaking in 1891, 'a tumour, an elephantiasis sucking into its gorged system half the life and the blood and the bone of the rural districts'. In the words of a report of 1908: 'London is being closed in. All round the country area, districts that used to be suburbs are becoming nothing less than great towns, and are cutting off London from the country.'

'Thirty years ago,' declared *The Times* in 1850, 'not one countryman in one hundred had seen the metropolis. There is now scarcely one in the same number who has not spent the day there.'

The Victorian Age of the Train – the first Underground Railway. Trial-Trip on the Metropolitan in 1863 (Guildhall Library, City of London)

In 1837 the stagecoach journey from Edinburgh to London took two days. At the end of the reign the same journey by train took eight and a half hours. Hotels were built at the terminals for the influx of visitors and tourists. The Great Western at Paddington was completed in 1853. Soon there were others at King's Cross, Victoria and St. Pancras. Then, away from the termini, came the luxury hotels: the Savoy (1881), standing on the site of John of Gaunt's palace, with D'Oyly Carte's Savoy Theatre close by; the Cecil (1896), to be demolished in 1930 to make way for Shell-Mex House; the Carlton (1899) and the Ritz (1904).

'The Tube' arrived on the London scene many years after the locomotive. Other 19th-century innovations did nothing to relieve the difficulties of traffic congestion. The monopoly of the hackney carriages, which went back to the 17th century, was challenged in 1829 by George Shillibeer's horse-drawn omnibus. His service ran from Paddington Green along the New Road to the Angel, Islington, then south to the Bank of England. With its minimum fare of 6d. (2½p), the horse bus, like the hansom cab, was used by the better-off. From the 1870s the working class came to rely on the cheaper, horse-drawn tram, which was banned from the City and the West End. By the First World War all forms of horse transport had been superseded. The future lay with the motor bus and, for a time, with the electrified tramway (first introduced in 1901 between Hammersmith and Kew). Above all, as was perceived as early on as the 1830s by a London solicitor named Charles Pearson, the future lay with the underground. London's (and the world's) first underground railway between Paddington and Farringdon (the Metropolitan) opened in 1863. The first electric railway in a deep-level tunnel (the genuine tube), going from the City to Stockwell, made its appearance in 1890. In 1900 the Central line opened, running from Shepherd's Bush to Bank. Quick to grasp the message, an American entrepreneur, Charles Tyson Yerkes, built the Bakerloo, Northern and Piccadilly lines, each of them making a right angle with the Central line.

*   *   *   *   *   *

About half a century later the tube stations became refuges. London's second great fire started at tea-time on Saturday 7 September 1940. At the start of the main target was East London and the docks. Thousands of East-enders went to sleep in Chislehurst Caves or Epping Forest. Then the whole of London came under attack.

Now began the period of sleeping in Anderson air-raid shelters, or on underground platforms; or of maybe dashing home before the black-out. Few people committed suicide – or got drunk – while the blitz raged. A communal anxiety, which drew people and classes together, helped to shelve the lonely and private despairs.

There were 415 air-raid alarms in that unforgettable autumn. By the end of September, 177,000 people were sleeping in the underground stations. Not even the tubes were safe, as the direct hits on Marble Arch and Bank savagely demonstrated, and six out of ten Londoners would stay at home at the height of the Blitz. On 15 October 400 aircraft came over by the light of a 'bombers moon'. An equal number of civilians were killed. But even these disastrous nights, when the capital was aflame, couldn't snap what Churchill called 'the tough fibre of the Londoners'.

From 7 September until 3 November the German bombers only missed one night. On the Sunday evening after Christmas (29 December) occurred the fierce attack on St. Paul's and the surrounding area. St. Lawrence Jewry and Christ Church Newgate were reduced to ruins. The Guildhall lost its roof. Miraculously, the cathedral survived. An incendiary bomb was lodged for a while beyond reach in the dome, but it fell outwards on to the Stone Gallery and could be put out. 'The dome seemed to ride the sea of fire like a great ship,' reported *The Times*.

On May 10 1941 the House of Commons was almost entirely destroyed. Members would in future meet in the Lords. Remarkably, Westminster Hall survived. The Temple Church, St. Clements Danes and Mercers' Hall were not so fortunate that night. However, the worst was over, at least for the time being. Raids became irregular after 16 May. However 1944–45 saw a further concentrated period of destruction, when first the doodle bugs and then the V2s attacked with horrifying effect.

Like Charles II during the Great Fire, George VI and his wife, Queen Elizabeth, didn't desert their posts, though they might have been killed, when Buckingham Palace was bombed on 13 September 1940. By their devotion to duty they won the approval of the Londoners. So did Churchill, whose wartime office in the thick of things, opened to the public in 1984, was beneath the Treasury Buildings in Parliament Street. The Citadel by Horse Guards Parade is a stark and sombre reminder of those dangerous times. The structure, which resembles that of an upturned ship, has foundations thirty feet below ground and several layers of concrete walls. In fact it is an extension of the Admiralty where vital wartime operations were planned.

By the end of the war 30,000 Londoners – almost half the total number of British civilians to lose their lives – had been killed and 50,000 injured. The loss of property was almost incalculably large. London received more than 12,000 tons of high explosives – on a provincial city, the maximum amount was 2,000. In Central London only one house in ten escaped damage. The City itself lost one-third of its buildings. Most of Wren's churches lay in ruins; so did the roof of Guildhall, and many of the halls of the ancient livery companies.

London had risen before from the rubble it would do so again. Before the war was over, two plans for London's reconstruction had been published. Their producer, Professor Patrick Abercrombie, had the radical vision of a Wren after the Great Fire. He saw much that was wrong in the metropolis 'obsolescence, bad and unsuitable housing, inchoate communities, uncorrelated road systems, industrial congestion, a low level of urban design, inequality in the distribution of open spaces, increasing congestion of dismal journeys to work.' Proposed solutions included ring roads, New Towns and, in London, the development of model communities. Ring roads would ease the traffic problem. Industrial congestion would be solved by moving industry elsewhere. Abercrombie's diagnosis was accepted by the LCC, though in the face of post war shortages his proposed remedies couldn't be implemented straightaway. However, by the end of 1951, the year of the Festival of Britain, over 40,000 new houses and flats had been built, mainly by local authorities. The regeneration of the South bank, proposed by Abercrombie, was inaugurated with the opening for the Festival of the Royal Festival Hall. In spite of prevailing austerity, and the more distant threat of the atom bomb, the future was faced with optimism, and this was expressed by the Festival, held exactly a century after the Great Exhibition. A year later, on the death of George VI, London embarked upon its second Elizabethan age.

Bomb sites gave way to skyscrapers. As the new reign progressed, the familiar landmarks, even St. Paul's, became obscured. New landmarks, like the soaring Post Office Tower and the long-empty Centre Point, a memorial to the property boom of the sixties, took their place. If Centre Point appeared to some as an unfortunate white elephant, there were other and brighter aspects of London's post-war evolution: restoration of historic buildings like Guildhall; a riverside development like Thamesmead; the South Bank, to which the National Theatre, long a dream, was eventually added in 1976, and, north of St. Paul's, where once a watch-tower (or barbican) guarded the approach to Cripplegate, the dominating Barbican complex, designed to make this section of the square mile once more a place where people might choose to live as well as to work. The wheel of the City's history has turned a full cycle; some are once again making the City their home, while others are renovating old houses in hitherto unfashionable areas close to the city. Perhaps they are all encouraged by the cleaner air which dates from the fifties when London was designated a smokeless zone. The famous smogs are now a thing of the past. This would have pleased John Evelyn.

The brash new world of high-rise flats and supermarkets isn't to everyone's taste. Perhaps the fast-disappearing back-to-backs had something in their favour – it must be pleasanter to design tower blocks than to inhabit them, as the planners themselves came to realize. Conflict between developers and conservers is only too familiar, and so it will remain while historic sites and old communities are threatened by the bulldozer. The controversy over the future of the Covent Garden site, once it had been decided to remove the market to Nine Elms, was one of the many rows occasioned by what for many was the mindlessness of the property man – if it's any comfort to that breed, Sir Christopher Wren also had his critics. Over the future of Covent Garden the conservationists won a major victory in 1976. By then the property boom was over.

While office blocks have proliferated, London's docks and

Proliferating office blocks in 1984 (Tom Picton)

traditional industries, which were closely linked, have declined or disappeared. Since Roman times, London has lived by producing, buying and selling. In the Saxon period, Cheapside, the main market, became with St. Paul's its very heart. In 1900 there were over 60,000 costers in London. At Billingsgate and Leadenhall Market, in Portobello Road and at the Smithfield Meat Market, in Spitalfields Fruit and Vegetable Market and, on Sunday Mornings, in Petticoat Lane, we may experience the essential flavour of the past. Tourism is the major industry of the present. The millions of summer tourists who thread their way through the pigeons of Trafalgar Square testify to London's continuing spell.

In the sixties a journalist coined the phrase, 'swinging London', but Carnaby Street and the King's Road are only one side of the coin. Blake's lines in his poem 'London' haven't lost their relevance:

I wander thro each charter'd Street,
Near where the charter'd Thames does flow,
And mark in every face I meet,
Marks of weakness, marks of woe.

The homeless and the badly sheltered, their ranks swollen by alcoholics, drug addicts, and human casualties of every kind, would provide abundant material for another Charles Booth.

London's imperial past has made London more cosmopolitan than ever. In the 1950's London Transport, anxious for cheap labour, recruited directly from the West Indies. Today the transport system largely depends on the West Indians. Racial tensions undoubtedly exist, and these can produce violence, or at least help to fuel it, though its scale wouldn't have greatly surprised the 18th-century Londoner. The Brixton riots of 1981 pale into insignificance by comparison with the Gordon Riots of 1780 depicted by Dickens in *Barnaby Rudge*. In Brick Lane, Whitechapel, the new Bangladeshi community has attracted the hostility which in the past faced the Irish and Jews. In medieval times, the merchants branded anyone from outside the city as 'foreigns' and 'aliens'. In modern times, however, small colonies of Poles and now Arabs in Kensington, Chinese in Limehouse and, more recently, in Soho, Italians in Clerkenwell, Australians in Earls Court and Irish in Camden Town, Kilburn and Brent – to name only a few – have won a greater or lesser degree of acceptance. Horizons have broadened by and large.

If Dr Johnson happened to return, he would be pleased to find his house in Gough Square carefully preserved as a museum. In Fleet Street, the dome of St. Paul's would at once tell him where he is, but familiar buildings would be few and far between. Yet neither German bombs nor the depredations of the property developers have destroyed the legacy of centuries. It is this heritage that provides much of the attraction of the present.

To Dr Johnson's intensely patriotic instinct, the 1977 Jubilee celebrations would have made a strong appeal. On 7 June a service of thanksgiving took place at St. Paul's. The Queen rode in state from Buckingham Palace to the cathedral. On arriving at Temple Bar, she touched the hilt of the Pearl sword – said to have been presented to the City by the first Elizabeth – offered by the Lord Mayor. The surrender of the City Sword symbolized her sovereignty over the City of London. The simple ceremony illustrates the direct relationships between monarch and mayor, who takes precedence in the City over all save the sovereign. When there was a gate, it was formally closed on the sovereign's approach, and the herald knocked three times before it was opened. Like the House of Commons, which still treats Black Rod in a similar manner, the City has never lacked a sense of its importance. So far as the world's financial affairs are concerned, this is not misplaced today.

Some Londoners watching the latest pageant could recall the Diamond Jubilee of Queen Victoria. These men and women had lived through a period of far more rapid change than any previous generation. Yet the government of the square mile remains proudly distinct from the rest of the London area. It had survived the creation of the London County Council in 1888. The Local Government Act of 1963, which created the Greater London Council, did not touch the City. Though London will go on being transformed, the City's independent traditions, which seem quaint and obsolete to the uninitiated, are almost sure to last.

Further Reading

London Life in the 18th Century Dorothy George (Penguin, 1966)

Dr Johnson's London Dorothy Marshall (Wiley, 1968)

Georgian London (Architecture) Sir John Summerson (Penguin, 1962, Barrie and Jenkins, 1970)

Hanoverian London, 1714–1808 George Rudé (Secker and Warburg, 1971)

London 1808–1870: the Infernal Wen Francis Sheppard (Secker and Warburg, 1971)

The Unknown Mayhew Ed. E. P. Thompson and Eileen Yeo (Pelican Books, 1973)

Charles Booth's London Ed. Albert Friend and Richard M. Ellman (Pelican Books, 1971)

London in the 19th Century Thomas Shepherd (Bracken Books, 1983)

Edwardian London Felix Barker (Lawrence King, 1995)

London Before the Blitz Richard Trench (Weidenfeld and Nicholson, 1989)

The Making of Modern London Gavin Weightman and Steven Humphries (Sidgwick & Jackson, 1983)

10 Historic London (4)

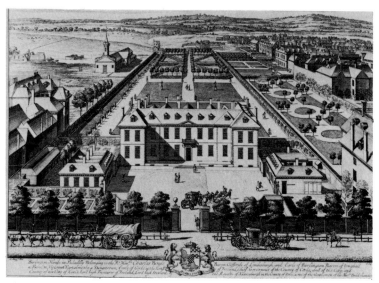

The first Burlington House, Piccadilly, 1707 (Guildhall Library, City of London)

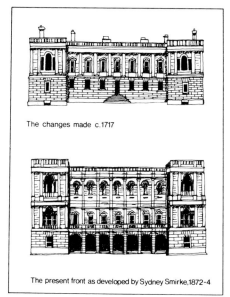

The changes made c.1717

The present front as developed by Sydney Smirke,1872-4

Burlington House 'palladianized' by Lord Burlington c. 1717 and later developed (D. Cheepen)

163

Burlington House

Lord Burlington returned from his travels in Italy fired with enthusiasm for the architecture of Palladio. Inigo Jones had experienced the same kind of conversion about a century before. With the single minded zest of a 22-year-old fresh from his Grand Tour he set about 'Palladianizing' Burlington House, built in 1665 on the north side of Piccadilly. The east and west wings, along with the statue-lined upper storey and entrance loggia, are 19th-century additions. The Royal Academy, founded in 1768, moved here in 1869 after spells in Pall Mall, Somerset House and the National Gallery.

The Burlington Arcade, a covered passage bordered with fashionable shops, was built in the early 19th century by the then owner of Burlington House, Lord George Cavendish, to prevent rubbish being thrown over the wall into his grounds.

Chiswick House and Hogarth's House

London's extending frontier meant that Lord Burlington's town house was soon no longer on the edge of the countryside, and a retreat must have seemed imperative. Chiswick House was modelled on Palladio's Villa Capra, near Vicenza. Lord Hervey said it was 'too small to inhabit, and too large to hang to one's watch'. The ground floor, which once housed the Earl's library, now exhibits drawings and prints on a Palladian theme. Mark the similarity between many of the rooms and Palladio's drawings of Roman baths. For the record, Charles James Fox died here (1806) and, in more recent times, this was a favourite resort of Edward VII.

The painter of '*Gin Lane* – the most graphic depiction of the degradation of 18th-century London's poor – was born at St. Bartholomew's Close within a stone's throw of Smithfield Market. Hogarth owned a house in noisy, bustly Leicester Square from 1733 until his death. The Chiswick home was his refuge. He died here in 1764 at the age of 67 and is buried in the nearby churchyard. The painter wouldn't appreciate today the proximity of the Great West Road to his once peaceful retreat.

White Lodge, Pembroke Lodge and Richmond Park

The park was enclosed by Charles I in 1637. White Lodge, on Spanker's Hill, has strong royal connections. Built for George II, it was the birthplace of Edward VIII and a residence of George VI when Duke of York (open occasionally). On the west side of the park the later Pembroke lodge (*c.* 1800), Bertrand Russell's childhood home, is now a restaurant. Also on the west side is the Star and Garter Home, occupying the site of the Star and Garter Inn, a resort of the famous and fashionable in the 18th and early 19th centuries.

'Too small to inhabit, and too large to hand to one's watch' – Lord Burlington's Chiswick House (Guildhall Library, City of London)

'Gothick' fantasy – Horace Walpole's Strawberry Hill (Tom Picton)

Marble Hill House and Strawberry Hill, Twickenham

Like White Lodge, Marble Hill House is connected with George II. This Palladian mansion was built for a Royal mistress. The furniture is of the period. Horace Walpole, Prime Minister's son, author and man about town, helped to plan the gardens. Walpole lived nearby at **Strawberry Hill**, his own creation in fanciful 'Gothick' from a cottage overlooking the Thames. Here he was inspired to write *The Castle of Otranto*, a Georgian spinechiller which would set a literary trend.

The Thomas Coram Foundation for Children, Bloomsbury

The Foundling Hospital for deserted children owed its existence to the determined campaigning of Captain Coram, who had been shocked by the sight of abandoned babies in the streets near his home in Rotherhithe. Its purpose was not just to save lives, but to save the children from growing into criminals and prostitutes. During Dr Johnson's time, the hospital became the dumping ground of all the unwanted children in England. Under such pressure, its efficiency tended to decline. Between 1756 and 1760, out of 14,934 babies admitted, over ten thousand died. This failure rate, which was bad even by 18th-century standards, led to a restriction of the intake.

From 1724 to 1926 the hospital occupied the site of nearby Coram Fields. The present house contains the Court Room and part of an oak staircase from the old building. Exhibited here are paintings by Hogarth, Kneller and Gainsborough, a cartoon by Raphael and a MS score of the *Messiah*.

Dr Johnson and London

'Three days I was upon the road, and the fourth morning my heart danced at the sight of London,' Dr Johnson wrote in the fifteenth *Rambler* essay. Though his heart may have danced, modest beginnings lay ahead. Even geniuses require a roof, and Johnson found one just off the Strand. Later, finding it difficult to work amidst the noise and bustle, he found lodgings in distant rural Greenwich. Then he came to live near fashionable Hanover Square. To the north, Cavendish Square was still unfinished amidst the fields.

Johnson eventually rented a property in Gough Square, off Fleet Street. The house, today preserved as a shrine, provided the setting for the compilation of the dictionary. Johnson, a constant seeker after mental stimulation, formed a club to meet every Tuesday evening at the King's Head in Ivy Lane near St. Paul's. Sir John Hawkins, the first major biographer, and one of the club members, described how his subject came from his labours to the King's Head. He was usually hungry:

> for our conversations seldom began until after a supper so very solid and substantial as led us to think that with him it was a dinner. By the help of this refection, and no other incentive to hilarity than lemonade, Johnson was . . . transformed into a new creature; his habitual melancholy and lassitude of spirit gave way; his countenance brightened; . . . he told us excellent stories, and . . . both instructed and delighted us.

In 1759 the expense of running an establishment in Gough Square caused Johnson, now a widower, to move into modest rooms in Inner Temple Lane – the dictionary had made him famous, but not rich. Four years later, James Boswell met the eminent man for the first time, in a bookshop at 8 Russell Street. Johnson's conversation would in future have a indefatigable recorder. The year 1763 also saw the founding of a new club, which met for a number of years at the Turk's Head in Gerrard Street, in Soho. It was a select band. When David Garrick came to hear of it from Sir Joshua Reynolds, the great actor remarked, 'I like it much; I think I shall be of you.' 'He'll be of us?' said Johnson. 'How does he know we will permit him?'

A pension from the King enabled Johnson to leave his chambers for a house in a cul-de-sac off Fleet Street called Johnson's Court. A month after the move, his eight-volume edition of Shakespeare was published – an immense achievement, which is naturally overshadowed by the dictionary. Boswell suggested that the doctor ought now to undertake a further major work. 'No Sir,' he replied, 'I am not obliged to do any more. A man is to have part of his life to himself.' Although the royal pension enabled Johnson to concentrate entirely on the art of conversation, contentment eluded him; the great lexicographer became obsessed with a fear of insanity.

In 1765 a new friendship developed. In January Johnson met the Thrales. Henry Thrale was the wealthy owner of a brewery in Southwark and of a country house at Streatham. His wife enchanted Johnson by her vivacity and intelligence. Their country house provided him with a refuge, while their company helped to lessen his mental torments. For many years he would spend the week with the Thrales, returning for week-ends to Johnson's Court, if only to keep Miss Williams, his housekeeper, and the rest of the household, company over Sunday lunch. Johnson was partially lost to the club, though Burke, Goldsmith and Reynolds were all invited to Streatham. Boswell was worried by the new development – was his biographical subject passing beyond his reach? Mrs Thrale was seen as a rival who must be outwitted. He took Johnson on an extensive tour of the Hebrides, where he enjoyed exclusive possession.

When Boswell visited London in March 1776, he found Johnson living at No. 8 Bolt Court, still off Fleet Street. This was to be the doctor's last home. On Mr Thrale's death in April 1781, his brewery was sold for £135,000. The purchaser was Barclay, a rich Quaker. Having, in her own words 'purchased peace and stable fortune', Mrs. Thrale married an Italian dancing-master named Piozzi, for which Johnson never forgave her. He was by now a sick man. 'The asthma is not the worst,' he wrote to Boswell. 'A dropsy gains ground upon me; my legs and thighs are very much swollen with water . . . My nights are very sleepless and very tedious. And yet I am extremely afraid of dying.' When his health briefly improved after his surgeon had drawn off nearly twenty pints of water, Johnson gave thanks for his recovery in St. Clements Danes Church. He wrote once that 'However bad any man's existence may be, every man would rather have it than not exist at all.'

After his death, Samuel Johnson was buried in Westminster Abbey, where many great writers have been laid to rest. 'Johnson is dead,' wrote Boswell. 'Let us go to the next best – there is nobody; no man can be said to put you in mind of Johnson.'

Dr Johnson's House (17 Gough Square) Dr Johnson lived here from 1749 to 1758 while working on the dictionary, compiled in the attic on the top floor. A window has been bricked up to avoid the window tax. It was here that Mrs Johnson died in March 1752. Relics include an early edition of the Dictionary and autographed letters.

The Cheshire Cheese (entrance, 145 Fleet Street) was a likely venue of Johnson, Boswell and Goldsmith. In Johnson's Corner there is a copy of a Reynolds portrait and underneath the inscription:

> The Favourite Seat of
> DR. SAMUEL JOHNSON
> Born September 18, 1709
> Died December 13, 1784.

In him a noble understanding and a masterly intellect were united to great independence of character and unfailing goodness of heart, which won the admiration of his own age, and remain as recommendations to the reverence of posterity.

'No, Sir! there is nothing which has yet been contrived by man, by which so much happiness has been produced as by a good tavern.'

Though Boswell doesn't mention that Johnson frequented the Cheshire Cheese, it's almost certain, given the nearness of his homes, that he did. We know for sure that he was a regular patron of the Mitre in Fleet Street.

Tyburn Tree

The prescribed penalty for most crimes in the 18th century was hanging. In London the chief hanging spot had long been at Tyburn. A hanging day at Tyburn (there were eight in the year) attracted as much interest as a modern football derby at Highbury, especially if a well-known highwayman was featured in the programme. All types of men were drawn to witness the spectacle, including the sensitive Boswell, who wrote in his *London Journal:*

> In my younger years I had read in the Lives of the Convicts so much about Tyburn that I had a sort of horrid eagerness to be there . . . Accordingly, I took Captain Temple with me, and he and I got upon a scaffold very near the fatal tree, so that we could clearly see all the dismal scene. There was a most prodigious crowd of spectators. I was most terribly shocked and thrown into a deep melancholy.

The condemned man or woman was conveyed on a cart from Newgate Prison, originally part of the gatehouse, now the site of the Old Bailey, to Tyburn Tree, which stood at the junction of what is today Oxford Street (then Tyburn Road) and Park Lane (Tyburn Lane). The spot is marked by a triangular stone set in the road by Marble Arch. In front rode the City Marshal while a company of redcoats marched in the rear. The procession stopped *en route* at St. Sepulchre's church, now the east end of Holborn Viaduct. Here the condemned man was presented with a nosegay, while the doom-laden tolls of the great bell quietened the hubbub. Further on, at St. Giles, near where Centre Point now stands, he was given beer.

The last Tyburn execution took place on 7 November 1783. Dr Johnson was sorry to see them go: 'Executions are intended to draw spectators. If they do not draw spectators, they don't answer their purpose. The old method was most satisfactory to all parties, the publick was gratified by a procession, the criminal was supported by it.' Some 200,000 had been drawn to Jack Sheppard's hanging in 1724, and even more to Jonathan Wild's the following year. With a pleasing touch of defiance Wild had stolen a corkscrew from the chaplain at the very end.

The backcloth to 18th-century Tyburn was the rampant criminality of Johnson's London which went unchecked by a police force. Horace Walpole, the Prime Minister's son, wrote that he never visited London without a blunderbuss – Walpole lacked the

Tyburn Tree – the execution of Lord Ferrers (Guildhall Library, City of London)

innate advantage of Dr Johnson's huge build. Though Johnson was in the habit of walking through the streets unaccompanied at late hours – possibly returning from the Mitre in Fleet Street or the Cheshire Cheese just off it – he was molested only once in all his time in the capital. On that occasion he put up a very stout resistance until the watch came to the rescue. This degree of immunity did not lead him to underestimate the hazards, which were vividly described in his long poem entitled 'London':

> Prepare for death, if here at night you roam,
> And sign your will before you sup from home . . .
> Some frolic drunkard, reeling from a feast,
> Provokes a broil, and stabs you for a jest.

Johnson may well have had in mind the mohocks, the vicious footpads against whom the nightwatchmen, the 'Charlies', were powerless. In the city's outskirts, the highwaymen flourished. The prototype of the faintly chivalrous gentleman highwayman was, in fact, far from typical. The majority were common rogues. They caused inconvenience as well as actual harm. A German visitor to London, named Kielmansegge, describes in his journal how he and his friends, who were on their way to a ball near Gray's Inn Road, took a long way around to avoid traffic jams but 'provided ourselves

171

The dignified Mansion House standing at the heart of the City (Guildhall Library, City of London)

with an armed servant on horseback, because my lady Huntingdon had been robbed a few days previously of her watch and money by a highwayman in those parts.'

The Mansion House and the Lord Mayor's Show

The Mansion House, built by George Dance the Elder, has been the official residence of the Lord Mayor since 1753. It stands at the financial – and vehicular – heart of the City. From here eight streets radiate: Princes and Threadneedle Street (heading for the north), Cornhill and Lombard Street (heading for the east), King William Street (leading to London Bridge), Walbrook (following the course of the lost river towards the Thames), Queen Victoria Street (to Blackfriars Bridge and the Embankment), and Poultry (soon merging with Cheapside).

Originally designed to 'show the new chief magistrate to the citizens', the great pageant in the City's year takes place on the second Saturday in November, when the Lord Mayor drives in his golden chariot to the Law Courts in the Strand, where he makes his final declaration to the Judges of the Queen's Bench. Then he returns along the riverside to the Mansion House.

Robert Adam and Five Stately Homes

Osterley Park House was originally built by Sir Thomas Gresham, founder of the Royal Exchange, in the 1560s. From that Tudor

172

The Adam portico of Osterley Park House with Tudor corner tower (Tom Picton)

Another stately Adam portico – Kenwood House (Tom Picton)

house the four square towers at the corners still survive. Within that structure it is the work of Robert Adam we see today.

Where **Syon House** is situated on the river side of the Great West Road, a nunnery was founded in 1415. After the Dissolution the property was granted by Edward VI to the Duke of Somerset, the same Duke who built the first Somerset House in the Strand. In 1603 the house was acquired from Elizabeth I by the Percy family, the Dukes of Northumberland. In the next century Robert Adam set to work, the grounds being laid out by the doyen of landscape gardeners, Lancelot 'Capability' Brown.

Garrick's Villa, Hampton, was the country home of David Garrick, actor and Dr Johnson's companion from Lichfield to London, from 1754 until his death in 1779. Garrick employed Robert Adam to remodel the house. He also had **The Temple to Shakespeare** built by him on the river bank.

Kenwood House, Hampstead, was remodelled by Adam in the 1760s, though the wings weren't added until the 1790s. This is the home of the Iveagh Bequest, a collection of paintings left to the nation in 1927 by Lord Iveagh, a member of the Guinness family. Don't miss the Library (the Adam Room) in the east wing. The Thrales' summerhouse, much used by Dr Johnson when he visited Thrale Place at Streatham, was moved to this estate in 1968.

Apsley House on Hyde Park Corner, another Adam design, was built in the 1770s. When presented to the Iron Duke, it became grandly known as 'Number 1, London'. He held annual reunion dinners in the Waterloo Gallery to commemorate the famous battle won on the playing fields of Eton. Close by, at the head of Constitution Hill, is the Wellington Arch.

Somerset House

Two bishop's palaces were among the buildings demolished to make way for the original Somerset House built by 'the Good Duke', Protector Somerset, in the reign of Edward VI. Stone for the purpose was gathered from St. Paul's Cathedral and from the priory of St. John's Clerkenwell. On Somerset's execution in 1552, the still incomplete palace became the property of the Crown. In the Civil war it became the headquarters of the army. Here Cromwell lay in state in 1658.

Sir William Chambers, architect of the second Somerset House (built between 1775 and 1779), designed a palace framing a courtyard. It was here that the Royal Academy had its second headquarters. On the west side is the 1856 extension of Sir James Pennethorne. The extension to the east, designed by Sir Robert Smirke and built in 1829–35, is King's College, part of the University of London.

The Principal Probate Registry in the south wing of Somerset House contains a register of wills dating from the 14th century, and it includes those of Nelson, Wellington and Dickens. They occupy six miles of shelving in the basement, and any may be inspected for a fee.

The records of births, marriages and deaths, which were in the north wing, have been transferred to St. Catherine's House, Aldwych.

The Bank of England and Sir John Soane's Museum

The history of the Bank of England goes back to the reign of William III (1689–1702). Founded in 1694 on the advice of a Scotsman called William Patterson, it was first housed for a year in Mercers' Hall, Cheapside, then moved to the Hall of the Grocers' Company (off the Poultry), moving again in 1734 to the present site in Threadneedle Street. The second building (1788) was intended by Sir John Soane, the architect, to resist riotous mobs, of which there were a fair number in the 18th century. (The legendary Gordon Riots had occurred eight years earlier.) The present edifice (reconstructed 1924–39) rises within Soane's outer wall with its imposing Corinthian columns. Look out for the Old Lady of Threadneedle Street in the pediment.

Home of a remarkable collector – Sir John Soane's Museum (Tom Picton)

Sir John Soane's Museum, Lincoln's Inn Fields, the architect's private house, has been exactly preserved in accordance with his wishes. Among the profusion of treasures which belonged to this compulsive collector are Hogarth's *The Rake's Progress* (eight scenes) and *The Election* (four scenes).

The British Museum

The wealthy Sir Hans Sloane died in 1753 at the age of 93. The origin of the British Museum was the purchase in 1753 of his library and collection bolstered by the Harley and Cotton collections of manuscripts and the Royal Library donated by George II. The exhibits were arranged in Montagu House, a building in the classical style, and opened to the public in 1759. Around the turn of the 19th century the Egyptian antiquities, including the Rosetta Stone, were acquired, and in 1816 the Elgin Marbles.

The growth of the Museum necessitated the present building, also in the classical style, erected between 1823 and 1847 on the site of the old House and grounds.

Holland House

This Jacobean mansion, acquired by Henry Fox, the father of Charles James, became celebrated during the time of Charles James's son, the third Baron Holland (1773–1840), when it was the out-of-town retreat of the famous and fashionable Whig set, Byron among them. One frequent visitor was Lord Macaulay, who wrote nostalgically: 'The time is coming when perhaps a few old men, the last survivors of our generation, will in vain seek amidst new streets and squares and railway stations for the site of that dwelling which was in their youth the favourite resort of wits and beauties, of painters and poets, of scholars, philosophers and statesmen.' Macaulay was unduly pessimistic. The east wing and the Orangery have survived. There is also a gateway designed by Inigo Jones. Surrounding the gardens is the wooded Holland Park.

Holland House – the favourite resort of the famous (Guildhall Library, City of London)

Clubland

Since the area between St. James's Park and Piccadilly, known as St. James's, was created in the Restoration period, it has been the preserve of the male sex. Here, from the reign of William III, many of the coffee and chocolate houses were established, and their successors are the private clubs of today. Here is a sample:

The Devonshire Club (formerly Crockford's), *the Mall* London's most famous gambling club, founded in 1827 by a fish salesman, William Crockford, who owned a shop at Temple Bar.

The Athenaeum, Waterloo Place Founded in 1823 for 'scientific and literary men, and artists', by Sir Humphrey Davy, President of the Royal Society, Lord Aberdeen (Prime Minister 1852–5) and Sir Thomas Lawrence, President of the Royal Academy.

The Reform Club, Waterloo Place Founded by Radicals and Whigs in the wake of the 1832 Reform Bill, it effectively became the national party headquarters.

Brooks, St. James's Street Founded in 1764. Until 1778 the Club met in the exclusive Almack's Rooms in King Street. It was the leading Whig club in the 18th century and the rival of the Tory White's. Charles James Fox used to gamble here.

Boodle's, St. James's Street Founded in 1762–4, it was situated here from 1783. Fox and Edward Gibbon were early patrons.
    Opposite Boodle's spot the 18th-century premises of Lock's, the hatters, and Berry Bros. the wine merchants.

White's, St. James's Street The oldest London club, founded in 1736. It originated in White's Chocolate House (1893). Early patrons included Jonathan Swift and Alexander Pope. Beau Brummell made its bow window the 'shrine of fashion'.

The Carlton Club, St. James's Street The leading Conservative club, founded by the Duke of Wellington after the Tory defeat of 1831. Like the Whig Reform Club, it resembled a national party headquarters. A famous meeting here in 1922 led to the fall of Lloyd George.

White's – the oldest London club (Tom Picton)

Keats Memorial House, Keats Grove, Hampstead

From 1818 to 1820 the young poet, a former medical student at Guy's, lived in the eastern half of the house when it was known as Wentworth Place. Fanny Brawne lived with her family in the western half. The Chester Room (not here in Keats's time) is a small Keats and Fanny Brawne Museum. The centre of Regency Hampstead's literary life was not Wentworth Place but Leigh Hunt's cottage in the Vale of Health. Here Keats met Shelley. Once, when walking across the Heath, he came across Coleridge, whose last, decaying years were being spent at 3 The Grove, Highgate.

Keats Memorial House (Tom Picton)

A Nash Trail

In an earlier age the area we call Trafalgar Square included the site of the Royal Mews. By the 19th century this was part of a squalid vicinity known as 'Porridge Island'. On John Nash's suggestion it was laid out as a square to improve the approach from Westminster to Charing Cross. The square itself was completed in 1841. Nelson wasn't hoisted to the top of his column till November 1843. The lions by Sir Edwin Landseer arrived much later (1867) and the fountains by Sir Edwin Lanseer Lutyens not till 1939. Just for the record, the column is 145 feet – two feet highter than the Duke of York's (1834) in Waterloo Place. No one can miss the four bronze lions. Less obvious are the four bronze reliefs cast from captured French cannon and depicting Nelson's four major triumphs – St. Vincent, Aboukir Bay, Copenhagen and Trafalgar. The square as a whole has a naval flavour with statues of Beatty and Jellicoe of battle of Jutland fame. Look out in the north-east corner for the equestrian statue of George IV, intended to crown **Marble Arch** in front of Buckingham Palace. This impressive entrance gate, designed by Nash, became a gateway to Hyde Park in 1851, and since 1908 has been an islanded gateway to nowhere.

The trail takes you through Admiralty Arch, a proudly imperial early 20th-century creation, into the Mall. To your right is **Carlton House Terrace**. The terrace, designed by Nash, stands on the site of Carlton House, where the future Prince Regent moved from St. James's around the time of Dr Johnson's death. The Ionic columns which once had screened Carlton House were incorporated in the building of the **National Gallery** – not designed by Nash – which dates from the 1830s. From the Mall (named, like Pall Mall, after the game of pail-mail, a 17th-century form of croquet) walk up the Waterloo Steps to Waterloo Place, thence to Regent Street, the route by which Nash connected Carlton House with the Adams' Portland Place and his own Regent's Park development, which starts, at the southern end, with Park Crescent and continues in the great terraces which skirt the park he landscaped. Alternatively, continue along the Mall with St. James's Park, also landscaped by Nash, to your left. Eventually a turning to your right, Stable Yard, brings you to **Clarence House** (next to St. James's Palace) which Nash built in 1825 for William IV when Duke of Clarence. Today it's the residence of the Queen Mother. Turning back to the Mall you will soon come to **Buckingham Palace**. In the reign of James I, the site of Buckingham Palace, at the west end of the Mall, was a

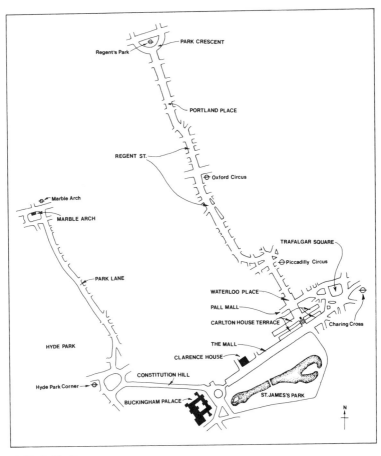

A Nash Trail

mulberry garden. The Earl of Arlington built Arlington House here in the reign of Charles II. Its successor, Buckingham House, built in 1703, was purchased by George III in 1775, some time after his famous meeting here with Dr Johnson in 1767. The building was remodelled by Nash for George IV who wished to make it his London palace, and since then Buckingham Palace has been the London home of the sovereign.

A barge on the Regent's Canal (Guildhall Library, City of London)

The Docks and Canals

The City of London had four deep-water harbours: **Downgate** (the mouth of the Walbrook), **Billingsgate, Queenhithe** and **Bridewell** (the mouth of the Fleet). The modern docks, which are artificial creations, were almost all built in the 19th century, in order to cope with the vast growth of overseas trade – and also to beat the many who operated illegally on the unguarded wharves between London Bridge and the Tower. London's first police force was not Peel's bobbies (1829) but the River Police formed a few years before to deal with the smugglers. Today the area is barely a shadow of its former self and the docks have been redeveloped for other uses.

Immediately to the east of the Tower, St. Katherine's Dock, whose foundations were dug out by Napoleonic prisoners, is now a maritime museum. The **India** (West and East), and **Millwall Docks** were on a neck of land known as the Isle of Dogs, drained in the reign of Edward II. On the south side were the **Surrey Commercial Docks**. Beyond Bow Creek, where the river Lea meets the Thames, were the

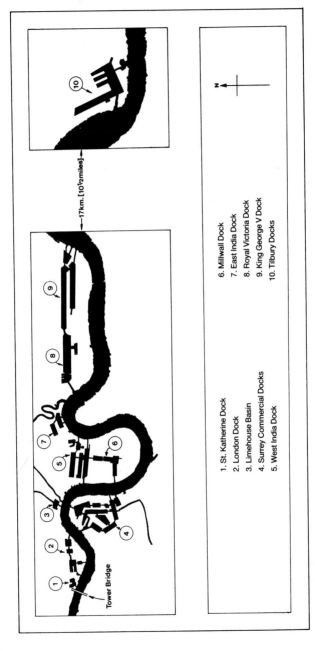

London docks

1. St. Katherine Dock
2. London Dock
3. Limehouse Basin
4. Surrey Commercial Docks
5. West India Dock
6. Millwall Dock
7. East India Dock
8. Royal Victoria Dock
9. King George V Dock
10. Tilbury Docks

←17km. [10½miles]→

Tower Bridge

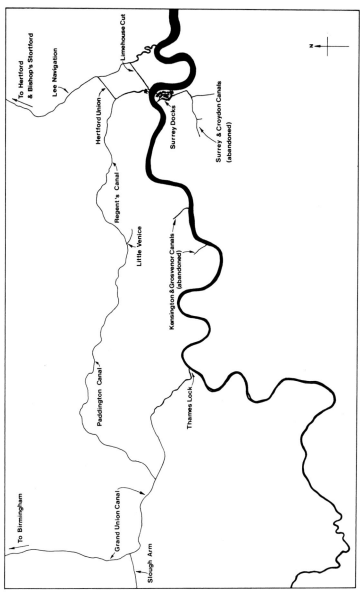

London's canals

three royal docks – the **Royal Victoria Dock**, the **Royal Albert Dock** and the **King George V Dock**.

A trip by motor launch from the Tower to Greenwich is a good way to appreciate the sadly diminished activity on the river, though the docks themselves are concealed from view. The Pool of London is the stretch of river between London Bridge and Limehouse.

The opening of the **Paddington Canal** (an extension from Uxbridge of the **Grand Union**) in 1801 transformed Paddington, where a large basin was built, into a flourishing inland port. The port belongs to the past, while the basin has been almost entirely obscured by the building of offices and factories on the wharves.

The **Regent's Canal** is a cutting from the Paddington Canal at **Little Venice** (so called by Robert Browning, who lived here), from where it passes through Regent's Park, Camden Town, Kentish Town, Islington, Hoxton and Bethnal Green on its way to the East End and the Regent's Canal Dock (now Limehouse Basin) at Limehouse on the Thames.

Dickens and London

The mean streets and fashionable squares of Victorian London were the inspiration of Charles Dickens. At night he would wander through them alone. By day his stored up impressions provided the raw materials of his art. Dickens and London are inseparable. His knowledge of it, like Sam Weller's, was extensive and peculiar. Like some other great Londoners, including Dr Johnson, he was not born there. In 1814 his parents arrived in London from a suburb of Portsmouth. They lived in Norfolk (now Cleveland) Street until 1817. After five years in Chatham, they moved once more to the metropolis, this time to Bayham Street in Camden Town.

When the family found itself in financial difficulties, Mrs Dickens tried to start a school for young ladies at 4 Gower Street. Charles was sent to work at Warren's Blacking Factory in Hungerford Street, now part of the site of Charing Cross station, and close to Hungerford Stairs from where the Micawbers began their emigration to Australia. Later, when Dickens was still employed, the warehouse was transferred to the corner of Bedford Street and Chandos Street, on a site later occupied by the Civil Service Stores. Dickens Senior, the model for Mr Micawber, was arrested for debt and sent to the Marshalsea Prison. 'Thirty years ago,' Dickens wrote in *Little Dorrit*, 'there stood a few doors short of the church of Saint George, in the borough of Southwark, on the left-hand side of the way going southward, the Marshalsea Prison. It had stood there many years before, and it remained there some years afterwards, but it is gone now, and the world is none the worse without it.' When John Dickens was released, Charles was allowed to complete his interrupted schooling at Wellington House Academy. Until its demolition in 1964, the house stood at the end of a regency terrace opposite what is today Mornington Crescent station.

Charles left school in 1827 to become an office-boy to a solicitor of Symonds Inn, from where he soon moved to Gray's. Later, following two years as a shorthand writer in Doctors' Commons, a legal office situated by St. Paul's cathedral, he became a parliamentary reporter. The reporter, turned humorous journalist, wrote *Sketches by Boz*, and then *The Pickwick Papers*, which made the 25-year-old Dickens a national celebrity. Following his marriage to Catherine Hogarth, he moved from his chambers in Furnival's Inn into a house in Doughty Street, Bloomsbury, which they left in 1839 for 1 Devonshire Terrace in Marylebone – now an office block. In 1851 they returned to Bloomsbury, where they lived at Tavistock House, today the headquarters of the British Medical Association. In 1858 Charles and Kate were divorced. Dickens stayed in Bloomsbury till 1860, when he bought Gad's Hill Place. Since boyhood, he had wanted to own this red-brick house standing close to the Dover road between Rochester and Chatham. Along this road the pilgrims had toiled on their way to Becket's shrine. Kate went to live in a house on the outskirts of Camden Town. On 15 March 1870 Dickens gave his last public reading in St. James's Hall, on the present site of the Piccadilly Hotel. He died at Gad's Hill on 8 June and was buried at Westminster Abbey.

The Deanery, by St. Paul's, was formerly the Vicar-General's offices of Doctors' Commons. The main buildings of Doctors' Commons, where Dickens worked as a shorthand writer, survived until 1939.

Wardrobe Place and *Burgon Street*, on the south side of Carter Lane, have hardly altered since Dickens knew them, when he worked in Doctors' Commons.

Johnson's Court, off Fleet Street It was here that the first essay, later included in *Sketches by Boz*, was pushed by Dickens through the letter box of the *Monthly Magazine*.

187

St. Mary in the Strand John Dickens and his wife were married here in 1809.

The Old Curiosity Shop, Portsmouth Street This shop claims to be Dickens's Old Curiosity Shop. However, the original of the novel stood near the site of Irving's statue in Charing Cross Road. 'One of those receptacles for old and curious things which seem to crouch in odd corners of this town.'

Dickens House No. 48, Doughty Street was the home of Charles Dickens from 1837 to 1839. Here he completed *Pickwick Papers* and wrote *Oliver Twist* and *Nicholas Nickleby*. Dickens House contains the best Dickens library in the world as well as personal relics.

Red geraniums, to be seen in the window boxes, were Dickens's favourite flowers.

Tavistock House Upper Woburn Place. It was here that Dickens wrote *Bleak House* and *Little Dorrit*.

Wyldes Farm, Hampstead Dickens and Kate retreated here following the sudden death of his beloved sister-in-law, Mary Hogarth, at No. 48 Doughty Street.

Eating Places Patronized by Dickens
THE CHESHIRE CHEESE Wine Office Court (off Fleet Street).
THE HORN TAVERN Knightrider Street, close to Carter Lane.
THE GEORGE AND VULTURE (in the Middle ages, **The George**) off Cornhill. An earlier patron was Dick Whittington.
RULES, Maiden Lane, Covent Garden.
THE GRAPES, Limehouse. (In Dickens's time **The Bunch of Grapes.** It has been identified with **'The Six Jolly Fellowship Porters'** in *Our Mutual Friend*. So has **The Prospect of Whitby** at Wapping. In fact the original was the demolished Two Brewers in Narrow Street, Limehouse.)
THE TRAFALGAR Greenwich.
THE SPANIARDS, Spaniard's Walk, Hampstead. 'All the way to the Spaniards at Hampstead' (*Pickwick Papers*).
JACK STRAW'S CASTLE, North End Way, Hampstead.

Southwark – some Dickensian and other Associations On the south side of London Bridge are the **Nancy Steps**, made famous in *Oliver Twist*.

On the east side of Borough High Street were famous inns known to Dickens. Some haven't stood the test of time. Near to the London Bridge end is the **King's Head**, once the **Pope's Head**. At the **White Hart** (which occupied the site between Nos. 59 and 63) Mr Pickwick first met Sam Weller. It had been Jack Cade's headquarters in 1450. The **George**, immortalized in *Little Dorrit*, is the last of London's galleried coaching inns. On the site of **Talbot Yard** stood the **Tabard Inn**, from where Chaucer's pilgrims set out along the Old Kent Road, which followed the course of Watling Street down to Canterbury and Dover. The **Queen's Head Inn** (marked by a plaque at 103) was owned by John Harvard, the benefactor of Harvard University. His fortune, of which half, with his library, was left to the university, was greatly increased by the sale of the property before his emigration to America. In Southwark cathedral a chapel is named after him.

Continuing south along the High Street, the wall of the **New Marshalsea** (the original Marshalsea, also in this street, is marked by a plaque at 163) overlooks Tabard Gardens to the north of **St. George's Church**, where Little Dorrit was christened and married. John Dickens, the model for Mr Micawber, was imprisoned in the New Marshalsea for debt in 1824 while Charles set out for the Blacking Factory from his lodgings in nearby Lant Street. Micawber himself found a 'temporary haven of domestic tranquillity and peace of mind' at the **New King's Bench Prison** at the north (Borough High Street) end of Newington Causeway. In real life, John Wilkes was imprisoned here for libel.

Part of the modern borough of Southwark is the former borough of Bermondsey. Here, at the east end of Tooley Street, lay the unsalubrious Jacob's Island, where Bill Sykes met his end in *Oliver Twist.*

The Albert Memorial, Kensington Gardens

Albert rejected a monument in his lifetime – 'It would disturb my quiet rides in Rotten Row to see my own face staring at me . . .' – but in death he could no longer object. Constructed by Sir Gilbert Scott on the model of an Eleanor Cross, it reminds us, as does the parish church of Kensington (also Scott), of the neo-Gothic revival. The monument is aptly located in the museum district whose development resulted from the 1851 Great Exhibition he helped to inspire – in fact a short distance from the site of Joseph Paxton's

Crystal Palace, built to house the Exhibition. This vast greenhouse structure, inspiration of I. K. Brunel's Paddington station, was moved to Sydenham, where it was burned down in 1936. In his hand Albert holds a copy of the Exhibition catalogue.

The Shaftesbury Memorial, Piccadilly Circus

The famous fountain, one of London's instantly recognizable landmarks, was unveiled in 1893 as a memorial to Lord Shaftsbury, the philanthropist. Its famous winged archer, popularly known as Eros, symbolizes the Angel of Christian Charity.

Booth's London

We went East along Brook Street, colour dark blue; rough, poor, many common lodging-houses, but no brothels. Then further East past the Friends' Meeting House to Cosh's Buildings, which fill the space between School-house Street and Collingwood Street, where Dunstan's Place used to be, and where that saint might well have seized the Devil by the nose. Here there are now three four-storeyed blocks. The centre one is very bad. Shrieks of a woman, who was being ill-treated, resounded as we passed through, and there was much excitement, all the women looking out of their houses; ragged, dirty, square-jawed women, and one was saying, 'she deserved a good deal, but I hope he won't go too far.'

Further on comes Causeway Court, a place not marked on the map, with drains chocked, everything overflowing into the court, and all windows broken – and so on and so on. But all is not bad in Weston Place – a cul-de-sac of three-storeyed houses, rough and dismal looking, with ragged-children playing about – a mite of eight or nine years was on her knees scrubbing the steps and the flags in front of the house. Dipping a rag and brush into the pail beside her as if she was fifteen, she called out, 'Look, mother, ain't I getting it clean?'

Charles Booth, *Life and Labour of the People of London*

Charles Booth embarked upon his mammoth investigation to refute what he supposed were exaggerated accounts of London's deprivation by Henry Mayhew and others.

Ironically, he discovered the problems were actually worse. About those whose way of life differed greatly from his own, Booth, like Dickens, possessed an almost insatiable curiosity. This, combined with a tireless capacity for work, produced the seventeen volumes of *Life and Labour of the People in London* (completed 1903). About a hundred years on, the findings have the power to shock, yet that power would have been infinitely greater had the survey been carried out a hundred and fifty years before.

Booth's 'poverty line' was eighteen to twenty-one shillings a week for a 'moderate-sized' family. Fortunate families within the poverty-line class would get by if they lived frugally. Below the line lay misery. Poverty and crime were bedfellows. It was in Shadwell, by the river, that Mayhew had convened a famous meeting of 150 young thieves. Jack the Ripper stalked in Whitechapel, leaving in his wake the mutilated bodies of prostitutes.

Booth's initial investigation, concerning the East End, revealed that of 900,000 people in the district, 314,000 were poor; that of these more than half were actually below the poverty line; that over half of these suffered from acute 'distress'. The cause of poverty was commonly low industrial pay.

In mid-Victorian times, London contained 15 per cent of all workers in England employed in manufacturing industries – no other city had so high a proportion. The vast majority were engaged in small-scale production – the census of 1851 records that 86 per cent of London employers employed fewer than ten men each. The inner areas had long been associated with particular occupations: weaving in Bethnal Green and Spitalfields, brewing in Southwark and Pimlico, sugar-refining in Stepney, clock, watch and instrument making in Clerkenwell, tanning in Bermondsey and biscuit making in Rotherhithe. Until 1867, when competition from the Clyde caused its sudden extinction, the Thames-side shipbuilding industry was a going concern. Nearly 6 per cent of all London males and over 8 per cent of all females were employed in the clothing industry. Most tailoring work was farmed out by 'sweaters' to people working in squalid conditions for small remuneration. Unpalatable facts in plenty were provided by Booth in the section of the survey that dealt with the Trades. The docks and tailoring were contributed by the young Beatrice Potter, the cousin of Charles Booth's wife, and later, as Beatrice Webb, a co-founder of the Fabian Society.

Booth's second volume surveyed Central and South London and

the outlying districts. Here, in supposedly the more prosperous parts, 30.7 per cent of all the people lived on or below the poverty line. There followed a series of volumes on industries, and in 1902–3 a further seven which discussed the influence of religion. Half a century before, when Mayhew had asked a costermonger what St. Paul's cathedral was, he was given the reply: 'A church, Sir, so I've heard. I never was in a church.' Booth concluded that London was 'a heathen city' in which the important influences were, not religion, but trade unionism and socialism. The movement founded in 1865 by his namesake he compared to a band of 'Ethiopian ministrels'! 'I have said that I do not think the people of East London irreligious in spirit, and also that doctrinal discussion is almost a passion with them; but I do not think the Salvation Army supplies what they want in either one direction or the other.'

Westminster Cathedral, Victoria Street

The principal Roman Catholic church in England and the seat of the Archbishop of Westminster was built during 1895–1903 by J. F. Bentley in the Byzantine style. The exterior consists of 12½ million red bricks (all handmade) with bands of stone. The campanile (284 feet high) offers a splendid prospect over London. Three domes rise above the nave, said to be the widest in England. The eleven columns of dark green marble supporting its arcades were hewn from the quarry used for the church of St. Sophia in Constantinople.

Markets

Petticoat Lane, Middlesex Street, E1. This Sunday-morning East End market, now well over a century old, was originally for old clothes. Today it deals in bargains of every kind.

Portobello Road, W8. This West End market, established in the last century, has long had two distinct fields of activity: antiques (on Saturday) and fruit and vegetables (Monday to Friday).

Westminster Cathedral – the Byzantine style in London (Guildhall Library, City of London)

The Ritz, Piccadilly

This dignified reminder of Edwardian opulence, decorated and furnished in the style of Louis XVI, was built in 1906 and named after its first owner, César Ritz, the son of a Swiss shepherd. The arcading at the front, which was to allow for road widening without the loss of building space above the ground floor, might possibly remind Parisians of the Rue de Rivoli – the Parisians, by the way, have their own Ritz Hotel. The restaurant, with its magnificent painted ceiling recently restored, offers both choice cuisine and a view over Green Park. There's the bonus of select company – some baronets, though rather more Americans, who dominate the Ritz's new aristocracy. 'The dignity of the Ritz has changed,' said a Ritz telephonist in 1981. It hasn't been entirely lost – you must wear a jacket even for afternoon tea, that relatively proletarian occasion.

The South Bank

Before the Second World War the LCC bought the land between County Hall and Waterloo Bridge, over the river from the City, for a south side embankment. When the site was prepared for the Festival of Britain in 1951, the clay was so loose that in some places the men had to dig 64 feet to lay foundations – pickaxes were quite close to touching the top of Bakerloo tube tunnel! The Festival Hall, erected for the Festival, is where the famous Red Lion Brewery stood. The Red Lion himself, once on the Brewery roof, is at the east end of Westminster Bridge.

The concrete jungle we call the South Bank is today London's cultural showpiece, though the Barbican Centre is trying to rival it. It was also for a time a major centre for skate-boarding! Accompanying the Festival Hall are the Queen Elizabeth Hall, the Purcell Room, the Hayward Gallery, the National Film Theatre and, east of Waterloo Bridge, the National Theatre – in fact, three theatres, with delightful music laid on in the foyer. If, when you hear the word 'culture', you prefer to reach for your knife and fork, you have plenty of opportunity, with two restaurants in the Festival Hall alone. Don't forget to linger at dusk over the view from Waterloo Bridge, or maybe from the Festival Hall during the concert interval. It has changed radically since Wordsworth stood on Westminster Bridge, and the ships, towers, domes, theatres and temples no longer lie open unto the fields, but the sight still touches in its majesty.

Edwardian Opulence – The Ritz, Piccadilly (Tom Picton)

Centre Point – a monument to property tycoonery in the 1960's (Tom Picton)

Centre Point

An interesting tale lies behind Richard Seifert's (now listed) monument to the property tycoonery of the sixties. In the late fifties the LCC wanted to build a roundabout at the intersection of Tottenham Court Road and Oxford Street. Inconveniently a property concern owned the required land. Then Harry Hyams stepped into the breach by buying it up – in fact, he bought up considerably more – handing all of it over to the Council and later renting back the area enlarged by land the Council had purchased. Part of the estate was to be for the roundabout (which ironically never transpired). On another party Hyams received permission to build his 35-storey block, worth about £17 million by 1968. It was kept empty while rents rose with inflation. Many years later, Seifert designed another colossus, the NatWest Tower.

Abbey Road

The Beatles spent far more time in London than Liverpool. If you walk up Grove End Road (on the west side of Lord's cricket ground) you will come to Abbey Road, where the Fab Four recorded most of their albums. Don't miss the zebra crossing, which was featured on the famous album cover.

11 London Names (2)

The following sample all originate since the medieval period.

ADELPHI	The Greek word 'adelphi' means 'brothers'. The Adam brothers created this fashionable terrace on the bank of the Thames.
ARTILLERY LANE	A shooting range used by the London Trained Bands during the lifetime of John Stow.
BELGRAVE SQUARE	Named after a village in Cheshire also owned by the landlord, the Duke of Westminster.
BOW LANE	Shaped like a longbow, this street was laid out in the 17th century.
CAREY STREET	Associated with bankruptcy proceedings, this street led in the late 17th century, when it was developed, to the home of Sir George Carey.
DENMARK STREET (Tin Pan Alley)	Named after Prince George of Denmark, Queen Anne's husband.
DUNCANNON STREET	One of the new 19th-century streets resulting from the laying out of Trafalgar Square. In 1837 the Chief Commissioner of Woods and Forests was Lord Duncannon.
ELEPHANT AND CASTLE	This important road junction south of the river was named after a public house. The present Metropolitan Tabernacle, that faces the junction, is on the site of the tabernacle in which C. H. Spurgeon preached from 1861 until his death in 1892.
FRITH STREET	This street in Soho commemorates James Frith, the 17th-century architect.
GRAFTON STREET	The Duke of Grafton bought land here in the 18th century. Previously 'Ducking Pond Row'. In medieval times, offending wives were ducked in ponds.

HATTON GARDEN	The house and gardens here were acquired by Sir Christopher Hatton, favourite of Elizabeth I. Now a centre for diamond merchants.
LITTLE VENICE	Opened in 1801, the Paddington Canal, a branch of the Grand Union, soon transformed Paddington into a prospering inland port. Little Venice, where the Regent's Canal meets the Paddington Canal, reminded Robert Browning, who came to live here after the death of his wife, Elizabeth Barrett, of a city associated with happy conjugal memories.
LOVAT LANE	Named after Lord Lovat, beheaded on Tower Hill in 1747 for his part in the Jacobite Rebellion. This was the last public beheading.
MANETTE STREET	Doctor Manette, in Charles Dickens's *A Tale of Two Cities*, lived nearby at 1 Greek Street.
MAYFAIR	This fashionable area, bounded by Regent Street, Piccadilly, Park Lane and Oxford Street, was for many years the scene of a May Fair in the late 17th century.
MILTON STREET	Named after the poet. Before 1830 Grub Street. Middle English 'grub' means 'a short dwarfish fellow'. Alternatively, after Grubbe, a known surname in Medieval London. 'Grubstreet. The name of a street in London, much inhabited by writers of small histories, dictionaries and temporary poems; whence any mean production is called grubstreet.' Johnson, *Dictionary* (1755).
NEW BRIDGE STREET	Constructed in 1760 over the line of the Fleet. It starts at Blackfriars Bridge, built to relieve the traffic congestion on London Bridge.
OXFORD STREET	This name first appeared in 1720. Previous names had included Tyburn Way, Road to Oxford, Road to Worcester and Oxford Road.
PARLIAMENT STREET	Connects Whitehall with Parliament Square, the Cenotaph marking the junction of Parliament Street and Whitehall.
PETTY FRANCE	Many Huguenot refugees settled here after their expulsion from France in 1685.
PORTOBELLO ROAD	A local farmer renamed his farm to celebrate the capture by the British Navy of Porto Bello on the Gulf of Mexico.
PORTUGAL STREET	Named in honour of Charles II's queen Catherine of Braganza.

PRAED STREET William Praed, a banker, was the first chairman of the Grand Junction Canal Company. The Paddington branch of the Canal terminates nearby.

ROSE ALLEY The Rose Theatre was the earliest of the theatres in Southwark.

ROTTEN ROW, HYDE PARK Rotten Row was the King's Way (Rue de roi) from Westminster and Whitehall to Kensington Palace. Rotten Row may be a corruption of 'Rue de roi'. Alternatively, 'Rotteran' means 'to muster'. This may have been a mustering ground in the Civil War.

SLOANE STREET, SLOANE SQUARE Named after Sir Hans Sloane, the benefactor of the British Museum, who lived at Chelsea.

SOHO SQUARE Before the Square was laid out in 1681, the fields were used for hunting. 'So-ho' was the cry of the huntsmen – the English equivalent of tally-ho. The Soho district, which lies south of Oxford Street, is a reminder that London has no need of the Liberty of the Clink.

WELL WALK The watering place in Hampstead was as popular as Bath and Tunbridge Wells.

WHITEHALL A term in use in the early 16th century for any grand hall designed for festivities.

WIGMORE STREET Named after Wigmore Castle, the seat of the Earls of Oxford, who owned the land here.

12 The Lost Rivers*

Names such as Fleet Street and Walbrook remind us of London's hidden or (in the case of Walbrook) dead rivers. The Walbrook, which once flowed through the heart of the old city, rose in the marsh called Moorfields immediately to the north of the city wall. One branch of the Fleet starts on Hampstead Heath just east of Jack Straw's Castle, then forms Hampstead Ponds before going underground. The other branch, starting in the grounds of Kenwood House, flows south to form the Highgate Ponds, then through Kentish Town. The two branches meet at the junction of Hawley Road and Kentish Town Road. Farringdon Road and New Bridge Street occupy the valley of the Fleet, which reaches the Thames just to the west of Blackfriars Bridge. The culvert may be seen from the Southwark side.

Early on all water was taken directly from the Thames and its tributaries, as well as from springs and wells, such as St. Pancreas's well, St. Bride's well and Clerkenwell, but the needs of an expanding population couldn't be met in this way, so in 1236 the Tyburn Conduit (pipe) was built. A banqueting house (now Stratford Place, off Oxford Street) marked the start. Other conduits followed. One supplied the Charterhouse. In the reign of Elizabeth I, reservoirs were built on the Fleet at Hampstead, but the major breakthrough was the construction of the New River. Today two-thirds of London's water comes from the Thames (above the town), one-sixth from the Lea and one-sixth from wells and springs, mainly in Kent and Hertfordshire.

The mouth of the Walbrook (Dowgate) was used as a harbour as early as Roman times. We find Henry II (1154–89) confirming the citizens of Rouen in possession of their port at Dowgate, 'as they had held it from the days of Edward the Confessor'. In later years the headquarters of the Hanseatic League was at the Steelyard, just

* For fuller information, see Nicholas Barton, *The Lost Rivers of London* (Historical Publications Ltd, 1982).

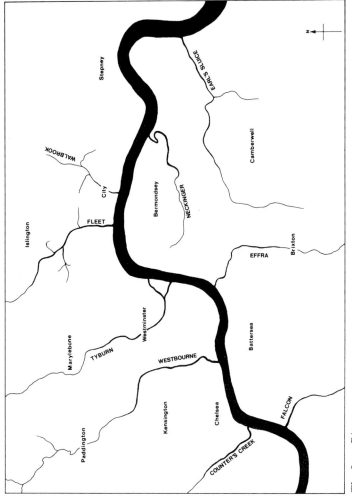

The Lost Rivers

east of Dowgate, on the present site of Cannon Street Station. Other deepwater habours in London were at Billingsgate, Queenhithe and Bridewell (at the mouth of the Fleet). The mouth of the Ravensbourne forms Deptford Creek, where Henry VIII (1509–47) founded a royal dockyard, later visited by Elizabeth I when she came to knight Sir Francis Drake aboard the Golden Hind. John Evelyn lived at Deptford at Sayes Court, whose gardens are today a recreation ground. After entertaining Pepys and Wren to dinner in 1671, he introduced Wren to Grinling Gibbons, who lived nearby. Gibbons's career was launched. When Peter the Great worked in the dockyard for three months in 1698, Evelyn let Sayes Court to him – a move he probably regretted for Peter left the house and gardens in a bad state. Czar Street recalls his brief and hectic stay. It was at Deptford that *Resolution* and *Discovery* were fitted out before Captain Cook's last voyage to the Pacific in 1776.

London's streams were a source of power. The water mills were used mainly for grinding corn and flour. Some, situated at the mouths, made use of the tides, an example being the mill which belonged to Westminster Abbey. Trades using water, such as tanning and brewing, were naturally sited along the banks of the now lost rivers.

Man has adapted for his edification what nature has provided. In 1730, at the suggestion of Queen Caroline, the Westbourne was dammed up in Hyde Park and converted into a curved lake, known at the Serpentine. The Westbourne, by the way, flows towards the Thames through that rectangular iron pipe which crosses the open air platforms at Sloane Square underground station. The lakes in St. James's Park and Regent's Park were created from the Tyburn. The lake at Kenwood, scene of delightful summer evening concerts, has been formed from the Fleet.

13 Population

U p to the first census of 1801 (recording a population of just under one million) figures are intelligent guesswork and vary widely. Roman London could have contained c.20,000 or as many as c.45,000. Before the 16th century, London may be equated with the area within the bars (e.g. Temple Bar). Once the era of rapid expansion begins (the Tudor and Stuart period), it becomes difficult to define geographically until the creation of the LCC (1889), which was succeeded by the GLC abolished in 1986. (There are now plans to recreate a strategic authority for the capital.)

The Black Death of the mid-14th century reduced London's population by about one-third, but thereafter it rose steadily. When Henry Tudor seized the throne in 1485, his capital city contained c.75,000 inhabitants. In the year of his granddaughter's death (1603), the figure, including the suburbs, was over 200,000. While the Great Wen continued to grow, the population of the City would eventually decline, a process hastened by 19th-century improvements in public transport, creating commuterdom. On Anne's accession (1702) it was c.200,000. In the year of Victoria's death (1901) this had declined to 27,000. In the same period, the population of London grew from c.50,000 to nearly 4½ million. In recent years the City's demographic decline has been reversed by the building of homes (many in the Barbican).

14 Famous Men and Women in London

Statues

BOUDICCA	Victoria Embankment
RICHARD I	Old Palace Yard, Westminster
ELIZABETH I	Churchyard of St. Dunstan's-in-the-West (originally on Ludgate)
OLIVER CROMWELL	Old Palace Yard, Westminster
CHARLES I	Charing Cross – here since 1675. Before the Civil War, in the churchyard of St. Paul's, Covent Garden. It was then hidden in the crypt of the church, seized by Cromwellians, and sold to a brazier, John Rivett, who disobeyed orders to break it up. After the Restoration he was persuaded to part with it.
QUEEN ANNE	Outside St. Paul's cathedral (another in Queen Anne's Gate)
WELLINGTON	Hyde Park Corner (another by the Royal Exchange)
VICTORIA	Kensington Gardens and on Victoria Embankment
PRINCE ALBERT	On the Albert Memorial (also Holborn Circus and by the Albert Hall)
WINSTON CHURCHILL	Parliament Square
FRANKLIN D. ROOSEVELT	Grosvenor Square

Addresses

PEPYS	12 Buckingham Street, WC2
HANDEL	25 Brook Street, W1

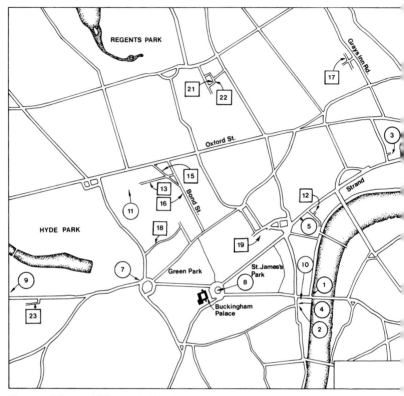

Famous Men and Women in London

DR JOHNSON	17 Gough Square, EC4 (see 'Dr Johnson and London' for others)
BLAKE	17 South Molton Street, W1
NELSON	103 Bond Street, W1
DICKENS	48 Doughty Street, WC1 (see 'Dickens and London' for others)
DISRAELI	19 Curzon Street, W1
GLADSTONE	11 Carlton House Terrace, SW1
WESLEY	Wesley's House, City Road, EC1
SHAW	29 Fitzroy Square, W1
VIRGINIA WOOLF	29 Fitzroy Square, W1
J. F. KENNEDY	14 Princes Gate, SW1

Statues – shown thus ◯
1. Boudicca
2. Richard I
3. Elizabeth I
4. Oliver Cromwell
5. Charles I
6. Queen Anne
7. Wellington
8. Victoria
9. Prince Albert
10. Winston Churchill
11. Roosevelt

Addresses – shown thus ☐
12. Pepys
13. Handel
14. Dr Johnson
15. Blake
16. Nelson
17. Dickens
18. Disraeli
19. Gladstone
20. Wesley
21. Shaw
22. Virginia Woolf
23. J. F. Kennedy

15 Twenty Tours of Historic London

Only the most dedicated will cover all the ground suggested. Those who do will have at the end some knowledge of historic London – and sore feet! You may prefer to appreciate London from the top of a bus – there is much to be said for this method.

The maps only cover essentials. An A–Z (look out for the de luxe edition) would be an advisable supplement. Use the Index on p. 243 to find the information given in this book on the places you visit. I strongly recommend membership of both the National Trust (0181 315 1111) and of English Heritage (0171 973 3400). In this way you both support good causes and, since membership provides free entry to their properties, save money.

On the oft-quoted Johnsonian principle, 'there is nothing which has yet been contrived by man, by which so much happiness is produced as a good tavern or inn', I include a number of pubs or eating places. Finally, remember that it is impossible for a London guide book to be completely up to date. Check thoroughly before setting out!

DAY 1

Underground:	Barbican (closed Sundays); St. Paul's
The Museum of London	Open Tuesday–Saturday 10 a.m.–5.50 p.m., Sundays 2 p.m.–5.50 p.m. Closed Mondays. Admission free after 4.30 p.m.
The West Gate of the Fort Bunhill Fields	Open Monday–Friday 12.30 p.m.–2 p.m.
Wesley's Chapel	Open daily 8 a.m.–6 p.m. House and museum open Monday–Saturday 10 a.m.–4 p.m. Admission charge.
Refreshment:	The Barbican Tavern and Restaurant, London Wall

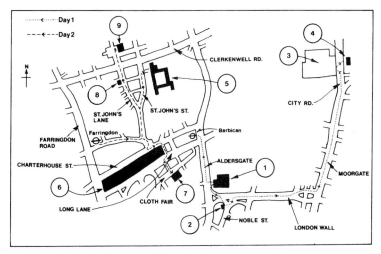

Route sketch map. Days 1 and 2

Day 1
1. The Museum of London
2. The West Gate of the Fort
3. Bunhill Fields
4. Wesley's Chapel

Day 2
5. Charterhouse
6. Smithfield Market
7. St. Bartholomew-the-Great
8. St. John's Gate
9. St. John's Church, Clerkenwell

DAY 2

Underground:	Farringdon
Charterhouse	Open 2.15 p.m. on Wednesdays April–July. Admission charge. (Or by arrangement with the master or registrar.)
Smithfield Market Cloth Fair St. Bartholomew-the-Great	
St. John's Gate, and St. John's Church, Clerkenwell	St. John's Gate museum open Monday–Friday 10 a.m.–5 p.m., Saturdays 10 a.m.–4 p.m. Admission charge.
Refreshment:	The Hand and Shears, Cloth Fair The Raglan, Adlersgate Street

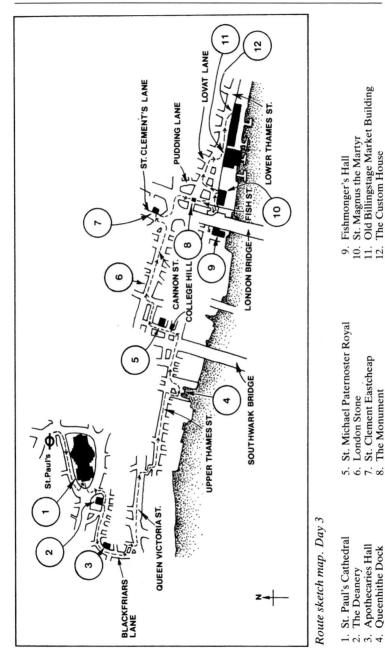

Route sketch map. Day 3

1. St. Paul's Cathedral
2. The Deanery
3. Apothecaries Hall
4. Queenhithe Dock

5. St. Michael Paternoster Royal
6. London Stone
7. St. Clement Eastcheap
8. The Monument

9. Fishmonger's Hall
10. St. Magnus the Martyr
11. Old Billingstage Market Building
12. The Custom House

DAY 3

Underground: St. Paul's

St. Paul's   Open Monday–Saturday 8.30 a.m.–4 p.m.
    Cathedral   Admission charge.

The Deanery
Apothecaries Hall
Queenhithe Dock
St. Michael
    Paternoster Royal
London Stone
St. Clement
    Eastcheap

The Monument   Open April–September weekdays 9 a.m.–
                        6 p.m., Saturday and Sunday 2 p.m.–6 p.m.
                        October–March Monday–Saturday 9 a.m.–
                        4 p.m. Admission charge.

Fishmongers' Hall
St. Magnus the
    Martyr
Pudding Lane
Lovat Lane
Old Billingsgate
    Market Building
The Custom House

Refreshment: The Horn, Knightrider Street
                        Ye Old Watling, Watling Street
                        Williamson's, Bow Lane
                        Old Wine Shades, Martin Lane

DAY 4

Underground:	St. Paul's

St. Mary-le-Bow
Goldsmith's Hall
St. Lawrence Jewry

Guildhall	Great Hall open daily 10 a.m.–5 p.m. (Closed on Sundays from October–April). Admission free.

Mercers' Hall
The Bank of
   England

The Royal **Exchange**	The Visitors' Gallery is open Monday–Friday 11.30 a.m.–2 p.m. Admission free.

St Mary Woolnoth

The Mansion **House**	Open for group tours Tuesday–Thursday 11 a.m. and 2 p.m. Apply in writing.

St. Stephen
   Walbrook
The Temple of
   Mithras
St. Mary Aldermary

Refreshment:	Williamson's, Bow Lane Ye Olde Watling, Watling Street The Three Crowns, Poultry

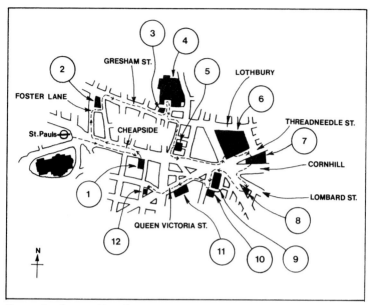

Route sketch map. Day 4

1. St. Mary-le-Bow
2. Goldsmiths' Hall
3. St. Lawrence Jewry
4. Guildhall
5. Mercers' Hall
6. The Bank of England

7. The Royal Exchange
8. St. Mary Woolnoth
9. The Mansion House
10. St. Stephen Walbrook
11. The Temple of Mithras
12. St. Mary Aldermary

DAY 5

Underground: Bank

**St. Michael's and
St. Peter's,
    Cornhill
Leadenhall Market
St. Andrew
    Undershaft
St. Katherine Cree
St. Helen's,
    Bishopsgate
St. Ethelburga,
    Bishopsgate
Middlesex Street**
    (Petticoat Lane)

**Spitalfields Market
Christ Church,
    Commercial
    Street
Flower Market,
    Spital Square
Return along
    Bishopsgate to
    Broad Street via
    Wormwood
    Street
The Dutch Church**

Refreshment: The Hoop and Grapes, Aldgate High Street
                                   The Clanger, Houndsditch
                                    The George and Vulture, St. Michael's Alley
                                   (off Cornhill)

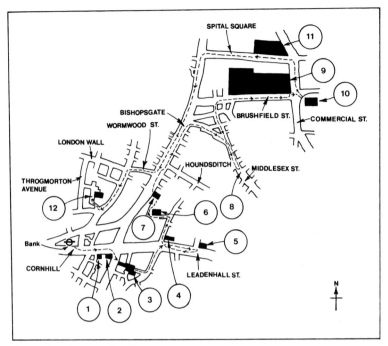

Route sketch map. Day 5

1. St. Michael's, Cornhill
2. St. Peter's, Cornhill
3. Leadenhall Market
4. St. Andrew Undershaft
5. St. Katherine Cree
6. St. Helen's, Bishopsgate
7. St. Ethelburga, Bishopsgate
8. Middlesex Street (Petticoat Lane)
9. Spitalfields Market
10. Christ Church, Commercial Street
11. Flower Market, Spital Square
12. The Dutch Church

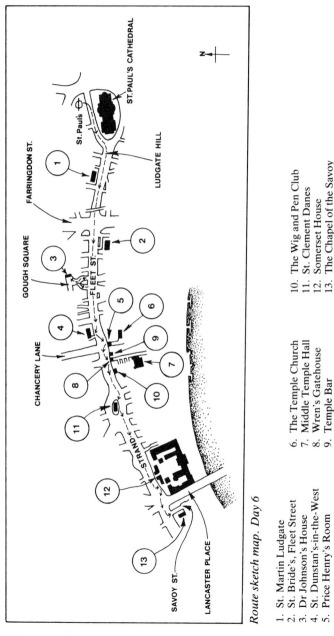

Route sketch map. Day 6

1. St. Martin Ludgate
2. St. Bride's, Fleet Street
3. Dr Johnson's House
4. St. Dunstan's-in-the-West
5. Price Henry's Room

6. The Temple Church
7. Middle Temple Hall
8. Wren's Gatehouse
9. Temple Bar

10. The Wig and Pen Club
11. St. Clement Danes
12. Somerset House
13. The Chapel of the Savoy

DAY 6

Underground:	St. Paul's

**St. Martin Ludgate
St. Bride's,
    Fleet Street**

**Dr Johnson's
    House**   Open Monday–Saturday 11 a.m.–5.30 p.m. (5 p.m. October–April). Closed Sundays and bank holidays. Admission charge.

**St. Dunstan's-in-
    the-West**

**Prince Henry's
    Room**   Currently closed.

The Temple Church

**Middle Temple
    Hall**   Open Monday–Friday 10 a.m.–noon and 3 p.m.–4.30 p.m. Closed Saturdays and Sundays.

**Wren's Gatehouse
Temple Bar
The Wig and Pen
    Club
St. Clement Danes**

Somerset House   Courtauld Institute gallery (only). Open Monday–Saturday 10 a.m.–6 p.m. Admission charge.

**The Chapel of the
    Savoy**   Open Tuesday–Friday 11.30 a.m.–3.30 p.m. Closed August and September.

Refreshment: Ye Old Cheshire Cheese and El Vino's, Fleet Street
The Clan, Mitre Court
The Deveraux Arms, Devereux Court

DAY 7

Underground: Chancery Lane

Staple Inn
Ely Chapel
Gray's Inn
Lincoln's Inn,
   Old Hall and
   New Hall

Sir John Soane's   Open Tuesday–Saturday 10 a.m.–5 p.m.
   Museum   Admission free. There is an excellent tour on
                    Saturdays at 2.30 p.m.

Underground: Covent Garden

St. Paul's Church,
   Covent Garden

Underground: Russell Square

The Thomas Coram Currently closed.
   Foundation
   for Children

Dickens's House

Refreshment: Henekey's Wine House, Holborn
                    Rule's, Maiden Lane
                    The Nag's Head, Floral Street
                    The Lamb and Flag, Rose Street
                    The White Swan, New Row

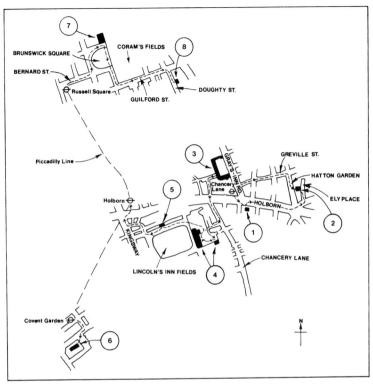

Route sketch map. Day 7

1. Staple Inn
2. Ely Chapel, Ely Place
3. Gray's Inn
4. Lincoln's Inn. Old Hall and New Hall
5. Sir John Soane's Museum
6. St. Paul's Church, Covent Garden
7. The Thomas Coram Foundation for Children
8. Dickens's House

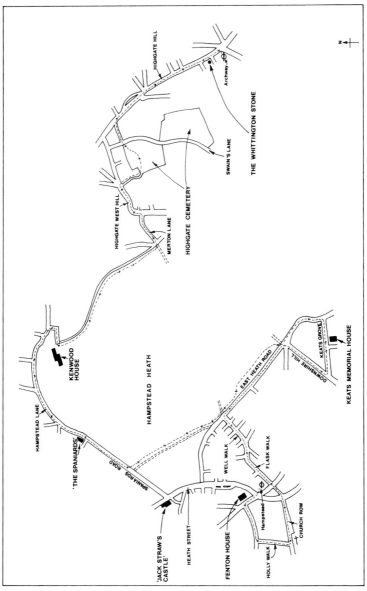

Route sketch map. Day 8

DAY 8

Underground:	Hampstead
Fenton House (National Trust)	Open (April–October) Wednesday–Friday 2 a.m.–5.30 p.m. Saturdays and Sundays 11 a.m.–5.30 p.m.

via
Holly Walk to
  Church Row

via
Flask Walk, Well
  Walk and East
  Heath Road to

Keat's Memorial House	Open April–October: Monday–Friday 10 a.m.–6 p.m. Saturdays 10 a.m.–5 p.m. Sundays 2 p.m.–5 p.m. November–March: Monday–Friday 1 p.m.–5 p.m. Saturdays and Sundays 2 p.m.–5 p.m.
Kenwood House (English Heritage)	Open daily 10 a.m.–6 p.m. (April–September) 10 a.m.–4 p.m. (November–January). Admission free.

Highgate Cemetery,
  Grave and Bust of
  Karl Marx
The Whittingdon
  Stone

Refreshment:	Jack Straw's Castle, North End Way
	The Spaniards, Spaniards Road
	The Flask, Flask Walk

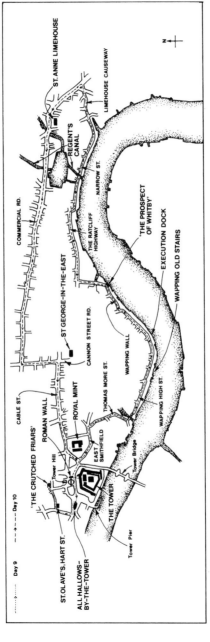

Route sketch map Days 9 and 10

DAY 9

Underground:	Tower Hill
Motor Launch:	From Charing Cross Pier
The Tower of London	Open (April–October) Monday–Saturday 9 a.m.–6 p.m. Sundays 10 a.m.–6 p.m. November–March: Monday–Saturday 9.30 a.m.–5 p.m. Sundays 10 a.m.–5 p.m. Admission charge.

The Roman Wall
All Hallows-by-the-Tower
St Olave's
The Bramah Tea and Coffee House
Butlers Wharf (by Tower Bridge)*

Refreshment: The Crutched Friars, Crosswall Street
The Three Lords, The Minories

DAY 10

Underground: Tower Hill

East Smithfield
Thomas More Street
Wapping High Street
Wapping Old Stairs
Execution Dock
Wapping Wall
The Ratcliff Highway
Narrow Street

The Regent's Canal
Limehouse Causeway
St. Anne Limehouse
St. George-in-the-East
Cable Street
The Royal Mint
The Tower

(A bus makes a circuit of the Isle of Dogs.)

Refreshment: The Prospect of Whitby, Wapping Wall
The Grapes, Narrow Street

---

* The Museum (opened in 1992) covers the history of the tea and coffee trade, which was so important to London's commercial development. There is an excellent cafe.

DAY 11

British Rail:	From Charing Cross to Greenwich or to Maze Hill.
Motor Launch:	From Charing Cross Pier (April–September).
The Church of St. Alfege	
The Royal Naval College	Open daily except Thursdays, 2.30 p.m.–5 p.m. Admission free.
National Maritime Museum	Open Monday–Saturday 10 a.m.–6 p.m. (5 p.m. in winter). Also Sunday afternoons.
The Queen's House	
The Old Royal Observatory	Open Monday–Saturday 10 a.m.–6 p.m., Sundays noon–6 p.m. (5 p.m. October–March). Admission charge.
The Cutty Sark and Gipsy Moth IV	Open weekdays 10 a.m.–6 p.m., Sundays and bank holidays 12 p.m.–6 p.m. (5 p.m. in winter). *Gipsy Moth IV* not on view in winter. Admission charge.
	From Maze Hill (on the east side of the park) a bus runs east to Woolwich. Another runs south from Woolwich to:
Eltham Palace, the Banqueting Hall (English Heritage)	Open Thursdays, Fridays and Sundays 10 a.m.–6 p.m. (or dusk).
Refreshment:	The Trafalgar Tavern, Greenwich The Yacht, Greenwich The Cutty Sark, Greenwich

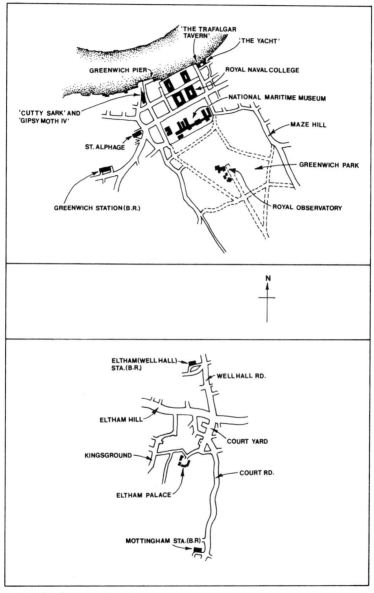

Route sketch maps. Day 11

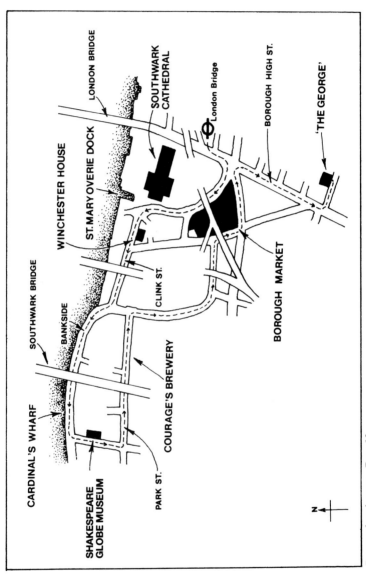

Route sketch map. Day 12

DAY 12

Underground: London Bridge

**Southwark
  Cathedral
Borough Market
via
Cathedral Street
  to St. Mary
  Overie Dock
The Rose Window,
  Winchester
  House
Cardinal Cap Alley
The Shakespeare
  Globe Museum**

Courage's Brewery Plaque marks approximate site of the Globe.

**Borough High   Spot plaques marking (1) the site of the White
  Street**   Hart, where Mr Pickwick met Sam Weller; (2)
                     the site of the Tabard Inn (Talbot Yard) where
                     the Canterbury pilgrims gathered; (3) the site
                     of the Queen's Head Inn owned by the family
                     of John Harvard; (4) the site of the
                     Marshalsea. Find a wall of Borough Gaol,
                     later the new Marshalsea.

Refreshment: The Anchor, near Courage's Brewery
                     The George, (London's last galleried coaching
                     inn), Borough High Street

DAY 13

Underground: Lambeth North

Lambeth Palace   Open by previous arrangement with the
                     Secretary (Conducted parties, usually on
                     Saturday afternoon.)

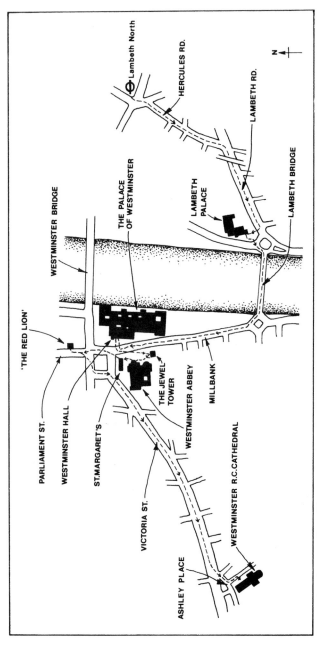

Route sketch map. Day 13

Lambeth North

HERCULES RD.

LAMBETH RD.

N

WESTMINSTER BRIDGE

THE PALACE OF WESTMINSTER

LAMBETH PALACE

LAMBETH BRIDGE

'THE RED LION'

PARLIAMENT ST.

WESTMINSTER HALL

ST.MARGARET'S

THE JEWEL TOWER

WESTMINSTER ABBEY

MILLBANK

VICTORIA ST.

WESTMINSTER R.C.CATHEDRAL

ASHLEY PLACE

The Palace of Westminster Open only by appointment with an M.P.,
Westminster except for the public galleries, which are
Westminster Hall open while the House is sitting. The queue
for the Strangers' Gallery in either House is
at St. Stephen's entrance.

The Jewel Tower Open daily 10 a.m.–6 p.m. (4 p.m. October–
(English Heritage) March). Admission charge.

Westminster Abbey Open daily 8 a.m.–6 p.m. except when there
are special services. On Sunday between
services only the nave and transepts may be
visited.

(English Heritage) The Chapter House and the Norman
Undercroft are open Monday–Saturday
10 a.m.–6 p.m. (4 p.m. in winter).
Admission charge.

St. Margaret's Westminster
Westminster Cathedral Open 7 a.m.–8 p.m.

Refreshment: The Red Lion, Parliament Street

DAY 14

Underground:	Charing Cross

The Banqueting House   Open Monday–Saturday 10 a.m.–5 p.m. Admission charge.

The Horse Guards Horse Guards Parade   The Changing of the Guard takes place at 11 a.m. (10 a.m. on Sundays). On the Queen's official birthday in June, the Trooping the Colour takes place on Horse Guards Parade, a gravelled space behind the Horse Guards.

Downing Street
St. James's Park
Marlborough House

The Queen's Chapel Open for Sunday services Easter–July.

St James's Palace   No admission.

The Chapel Royal   Open for services when the Queen's Chapel is not in use.

Clarence House   No admission.

The Ritz Hotel
Burlington House   Open for annual summer exhibition May–August, and for other exhibitions throughout the year. Admission charge.

St James's Church, Piccadilly
The Duke of York's Column

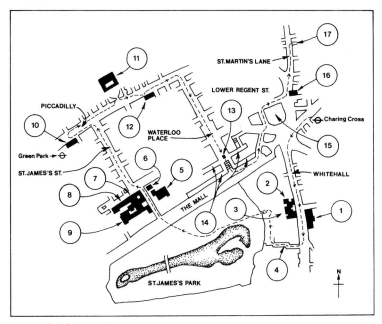

Route sketch map. Day 14

1. The Banqueting House
2. The Horse Guards
3. Horse Guards Parade
4. Downing Street
5. Marlborough House
6. The Queen's Chapel
7. St. James's Palace
8. The Chapel Royal
9. Clarence House

10. The Ritz Hotel
11. Burlington House
12. St. James's Church, Piccadilly
13. The Duke of York's Column
14. Carlton House Terrace
15. Trafalgar Square
16. St. Martin's-in-the-Fields
17. Goodwin's Court

Carlton House Terrace
Trafalgar Square
St. Martin's-in-the-Fields
Goodwin's Court

Refreshment: The Architectural Press and The Two Chairmen, Queen Anne's Gate

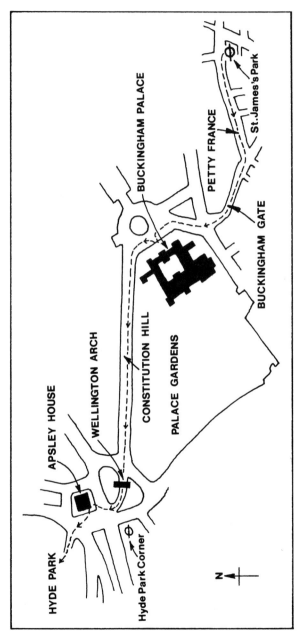

Route sketch map. Day 15

DAY 15

Underground: St James's Park

Buckingham Palace Open daily August–October 9.30 a.m.–4.30 p.m. Admission charge. (Ticket Office is located in Green Park.)

THE QUEEN'S GALLERY Open Tuesday–Saturday 10 a.m.–5 p.m. Sundays 2 p.m.–5 p.m. Admission charge.

THE ROYAL MEWS Open Tuesday–Thursday noon–4 p.m. (On Wednesdays only in winter). Admission charge.

Wellington Arch
Apsley House   Open Tuesday–Sunday, 11 a.m.–5 p.m. Admission charge.

Hyde Park

Refreshment: The Colonies, Wilfred Street
The Albert, Victoria Street

DAY 16

Underground:	Ladbrooke Grove

Portobello Road
Kensington Palace Open May–September for guided tours (charge). Monday–Saturday 9.30 a.m.–3.30 p.m. (from 11.30 a.m. on Sundays).

Underground: Holland Park

Holland House

Underground: Putney Bridge

Fulham Palace

Crosby Hall Ring for admission

Carlyle's House Open April–October Wednesday–Sunday
  (National Trust) 11 a.m.–5 p.m. Admission charge.

The Royal Hospital Open Monday–Saturday 10 a.m.–noon, 2 p.m.–4 p.m. Admission charge. Sundays 2 p.m.–4 p.m. (free).

Refreshment: The King's Head and Eight Bells, Cheyne Walk

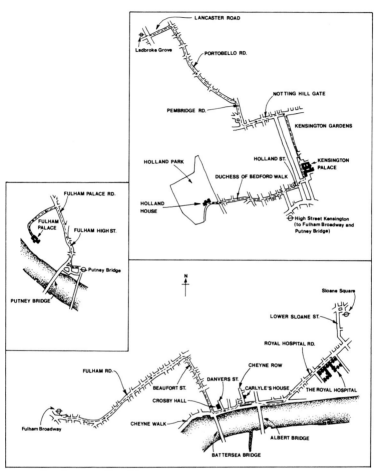

Route sketch maps. Day 16

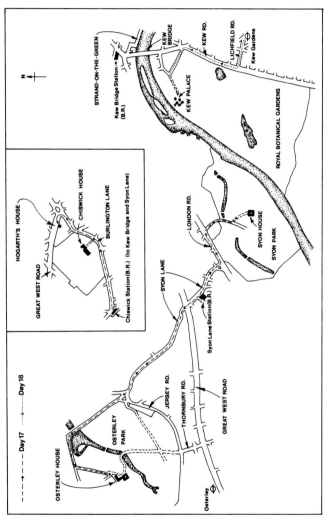

Route sketch maps. Days 17 and 18

DAY 17

British Rail:	From Waterloo to Chiswick
Chiswick House (English Heritage)	Open daily 10 a.m.–6 p.m. (April–September). Wednesday–Sunday 10 a.m.–4 p.m. (October–March). Admission charge.
Hogarth's House	Open 11 a.m.–6 p.m. Monday–Saturday, except Tuesdays (April–September). 11 a.m.–4 p.m. (October–March). Sundays from 2 p.m. Closed first two weeks in September and last three weeks in December. Admission free.
British Rail:	From Kew Bridge to Syon Lane
Syon House	Open April–September, Wednesday–Sunday 11 a.m.–5 p.m. Sundays only in October. Admission charge. The park is open daily till dusk. Admission charge.
Osterley Park House (National Trust)	Open April–October, Wednesday–Sunday 11 a.m.–5 p.m. Admission charge. The grounds are open daily till dusk.
Refreshment:	The City Barge, Strand on the Green

DAY 18

Underground:	Kew Gardens
Kew Palace and Gardens	Palace open daily April–September 11 a.m.–5.30 p.m. Admission charge. The gardens are open daily till dusk.
Refreshment:	The London Apprentice, Isleworth

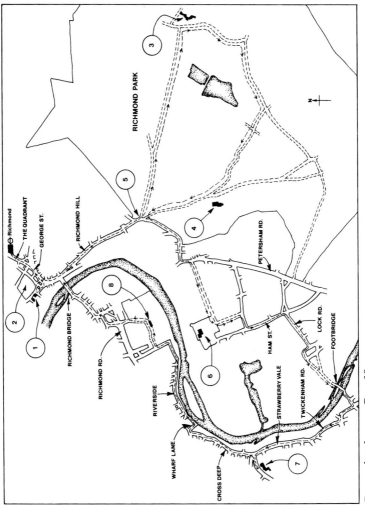

1. Richmond Palace
2. Richmond Green
3. White Lodge
4. Pembroke Lodge
5. Richmond Gate
6. Ham House
7. Strawberry Hill
8. Marble Hill House

Route sketch map. Day 19

DAY 19

Underground:	Richmond Station
British Rail:	From Waterloo
Motor Launch:	From Westminster Pier (April–September)

Richmond Palace
Richmond Green
White Lodge   Closed to the public

Pembroke Lodge   Now a tea house, open daily except November and December when Saturday and Sunday only.

Leave the park by RICHMOND GATE. Take the road to Kingston.

Ham House
(National Trust)   Open April–September, Monday–Wednesday 11 a.m.–5 p.m., 11 a.m.–5.30 p.m. (Saturday). 11.30 a.m.–5.30 p.m. (Sunday). November–March, Saturday and Sunday only. Admission charge.

Strawberry Hill   Open April–October, Sunday 2 p.m.–4.30 p.m. (Rest of the year by appointment).

Marble Hill House
(English Heritage)   Open April–October daily y10 a.m.–6 p.m. November–March: Wednesday–Sunday 10 a.m.–4 p.m. Admission charge.

Refreshment: The Cricketers, Richmond Green
The White Swan, Old Palace Lane
The White Cross, Water Lane

DAY 20

British Rail:	From Waterloo to Hampton Court
Motor Launch:	From Westminster Pier (April–September)

Hampton Court Palace — Open daily 9.30 a.m.–6 p.m. Admission charge. The grounds are open till dusk. Admission free.

Garrick's Villa and Temple to Shakespeare

Refreshment: The Bell, East Molesey

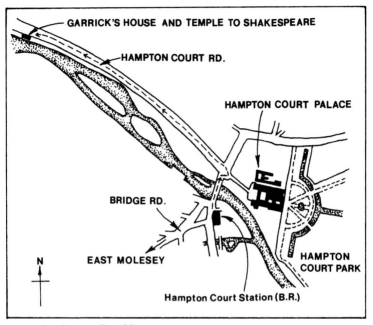

Route sketch map. Day 20

Note

There is now the London For Less discount card, sold at London Tourist Board offices. (The main central office is in the forecourt of Victoria Station). This gives you up to £2 off selected sights, discounts at certain shops, and twenty five percent off your bill in various restaurants and theatres.

Other walking tours are detailed weekly in *Time Out*. Two walking tour companies:

Original London Walks (0171 624 3978).
　The widest range of walks.

Historical Tours (0181 668 4019).
　Covers the City and Westminster, and also offers evening pub walks.

The flow of general books on London since 1984 includes:

History

The London Encyclopaedia, Weinreb and Hibbert (Papermac, 1987)
London. A Companion to its History and Archaeology, Malcolm
　　　　Billings (Kyle Cathie Ltd, 1994)
London. A Social History, Roy Porter (Penguin, 1996)

Guides

London under London: a subterranean guide, Trench and Hillman
　　　　(John Murray, 1985)
London Step by Step, Christopher Turner (Pan, 1985)
The Art and Architecture of London, Anne Saunders (Phaidon Press,
　　　　1987)
London Louise Nicholson's definitive guide, (Michael Joseph, 1988)
　　　　Now Fodor's London Companion
London. The Rough Guide, Rob Humphreys (1997)
Eyewitness Travel Guides London, Michael Leapman (Dorling
　　　　Kindersley, 1997)
Walking London, Andrew Duncan (New Holland, 1997)

Index